W9-AHU-638

JAN   2002

MY FATHER'S CABIN

MY FATHER'S CABIN

MARK PHILLIPS

THE LYONS PRESS

Guilford, Connecticut

An Imprint of The Globe Pequot Press

Copyright © 2001 by Mark Phillips

ALL RIGHTS RESERVED. No part of this book may be reproduced or transmitted in any form by any means, electronic or mechanical, including photocopying and recording, or by any information storage and relevant system, except as may be expressly permitted by the 1976 Copyright Act or in writing from the publisher. Requests for permission should be addressed to The Globe Pequot Press, P.O. Box 480, Guilford, CT 06437.

The Lyons Press is an imprint of The Globe Pequot Press.

Printed in the United States of America

10 9 8 7 6 5 4 3 2 1

Design by Compset, Inc.

Library of Congress Cataloging-in-Publication Data is available on file.

ISBN 1-58574-391-7

For Eva and Margaret Phillips
and in memory of James and Alfred Phillips

It is a rich hour of mammalian desire—a phantasy of Nature—godson, let us disport in dulcet leisure and leave behind Job! Job! Job!

—Pietro di Donato,
Christ in Concrete

ACKNOWLEDGMENTS

For their generous support and encouragement, I wish to thank Bill Goodman, Chris Pavone, Amanda Murray, Colleen Taggerty, Cass Ray, Anonymous Donor, and especially Hope and Gabriel Phillips. Thanks also to the Vogelstein Foundation and to my helpful and patient editors at publications where portions of this book have appeared: *The New York Times Magazine, North Dakota Quarterly, Notre Dame Magazine*, and *The Sun*.

And a note on spelling

The place-name Allegheny sometimes appears in this memoir as *Allegany*. The author lives in the hills of the Allegheny Plateau and near the river and national forest given the name Allegheny, but also lives near the town, county, state park, and Native American reservation given the name Allegany, a regional variation of Allegheny.

CONTENTS

The Lay of the Land

With a map spread before him at the kitchen table, my father seemed a dream of the misty Alleghenies. He took a deep drag on his cigarette and appeared to me behind the smoke of his chant: Munger Hollow Kinney Hollow Skunk Hollow Salt Rising Road Promised Land Road Stony Lonesome Road Great Valley Little Valley Starvation Hill Bear Creek Wolf Creek Trapping Brook Hanging Bog Town of Kill Buck. He told me his favorite place in the Alleghenies was a trout stream with the Indian name of Ischua: he said he didn't know what the name meant in the Seneca language, but that if I listened carefully I could hear the water in *"ISHooway."* I tried. And though I couldn't hear the water, I said I could. He smiled and told me about the glaciers that had gouged the hollows and valleys, about the wolves that must have denned near Wolf Creek, and about the lives of pioneers, the Mungers and Kinneys, whose names survive on maps but no longer on their weathered gravestones. He punctuated his excitement with drags of smoke and gulps of beer—and like a toddler learning to speak, longing to please, I searched in stumbling whispers: *"ISH-oo-way, ISH-oo-way."* I tried speed: *"ISHooway ISHooway ISHooway—"*

"You like that name? You can hear the water?"

I wasn't sure yet. I nodded.

He nodded and grinned and said, "Mark, go get me another beer; would ya?"

I fetched a brown bottle from the cardboard case on the porch—he liked his beer warm—and when I reentered the kitchen I could hear that in the living room Walter Cronkite had signed off and the shows had started. Yet my father was still sitting at the table in a cloud of smoke, studying a map and ready to talk some more.

Normally when he returned home from the power plant—still hearing the high deafening whine of turbines and the pounding rattle of coal dropping through chutes—all he wanted to do was eat supper, loll in his easy chair, smoke and drink, and fall asleep while the television blared. And yet when I handed him the bottle of Genesee and began to turn away, eager to join my mother and sisters in front of the television, he quickly motioned me back into a chair at the table to hear more mapped tales. I dutifully sat, and listened.

A few days later at supper, he announced that he planned to stop working so much overtime at the plant. Also that he had all but decided to buy some land on the Allegheny Plateau where the glaciated hills knuckled across the Pennsylvania border into the high dairy country of southwestern New York: "Land with a good spring so we can have clean drinking water and a trout pond. A place where we can build a little cabin. Where we can all spend summer weekends and where Mark and me can stay in deer season."

He had often talked about buying land in those rugged hills south of our home near Buffalo, but this time he spoke with more longing than usual, and I can still see his hands motioning as he seemed to plead, nails black with grease and coal, his wrists scabbed and scarred from the molten metal of welding, uncharacteristically punctuating his speech as he groped for the words that might help us to see his dream. For a few moments after falling quiet, he continued awkwardly gesturing.

Kim asked if the bugs would be bad in the woods. April asked if there would be bears. And I asked how good the television reception would be so far from Buffalo. Mom stood up and began clearing the table, the silverware and dishes clattering louder than usual. Looking down at his plate as if ashamed, he added quietly, "It's been a dream of mine."

A map can show you where you've been and where you intend to go, but not if you'll get there or what will happen if you do: it tells a story in the past tense. That evening when my father was possessed by a map at the kitchen table, he could see the routes from wilderness to settlement, could trace the stories of the cougar and bear and wolf and beaver and elk and the great forest and the legends of the thirsty men who felled trees, slew beasts, broke soil. He could see the routes he himself had traced to steep hillsides where he had searched for a gushing spring that would quench his coal-dusty thirst. In the place names, he might have seen the claims that people make on the land; and in the symbols for cemeteries, the claims that the land makes on people. But on his map, he could not yet dream the end of his own story.

That the land would dream.

———◆◆◆———

Imagine a dream that's also a real place, a forested hilltop above Ischua Creek on a muggy afternoon in 1792—one of countless crests among forested hills rolling to the horizon like waves on a green sea—as the land-company crew begins unpacking and attacking their lunches of salt pork and fried bread. Sitting Indian-style on the leafy ground, swatting at deer flies, the head surveyor drafts yet another line on the working map of the newly designated Lot 32 of Township 3 and Range 3, chewing the dry stringy meat as he works in a dirty folio that is becoming dotted with his sweat. Most of the crew are too hungry to even talk, but one of the axmen, who seldom converses even if he has been drinking spirits, mounts a horse, his lunch still packed. The head surveyor looks up to say something, but then merely watches as the axman rides off into the woods.

The axman hasn't gone far, over a sudden dip that hides him from their view, when he smiles at hearing a few of the crew make their predictably piti-ful imitations of howling wolves and screeching Indians. He knows well that not many miles from here, the Seneca, allied with the British during the War for Independence, captured a patriot and lashed him pleading to a young oak. They made a small slit in his abdomen and tied a length of intestine to the tree and forced him to run screaming 'round and 'round until disembow-eled he was left to die alone in a tangled heap of himself. Not to be outdone, one of General Sullivan's troops later made leggings from the skin of a freshly slain Seneca warrior. The axman also knows that on remote Al-legheny reservations the defeated Seneca are now starving and diseased and drunk and converting to Christianity too late to be saved. Wolves, though, he has seen almost daily.

The maple and scattered elm and ash are straight and tall, and the beech broad and gnarled. The horse is more hindered by the thick mossy boles of windfalls than by the thin undergrowth of the forest. Twice he dismounts and digs into the earth. This is not the lot he will buy with his earnings from the Holland Land Company, the soil too shallow and stony. But eventually some other land-starved man will buy it on credit, pick it from a map at the urging of a Holland Land Company agent who will tell the aspiring pioneer whatever he wishes to hear.

The sweaty axman dismounts at a gushing spring, and on his hands and knees sips clear icy water off smooth stones. He decides to eat his lunch there, where he can forget about danger and ease his exhaustion. Already some of the crew have abandoned the job and returned home after too many weeks of mud and rain and fording freezing streams and climbing steep mountains; too many weeks of the tearing briars of tangled deadfalls; too many weeks of fitful sleep on hard ground while wolves howl and cougars snarl in the darkness; too many weeks of hungry mosquitoes and flies. The axman is certain that many of the first settlers will also quit, defeated by the land and lonely for family and comforts left behind. But he himself so likes the outdoors and dislikes human company that he enjoys eating his lunch alone in the wilderness and rarely thinks about home.

How many years has he dreamed of this? He smiles and leans back against the smooth bark of a wide beech, gulps his food, closes his weary eyes, listens to pristine water rise gurgling from deep within the earth, and feels himself imagined.

The Stories They Told

Coughing men stripped the black seams of Ohio and Kentucky, heaped full the platters of long trains and trucks and lake freighters, and sent the dusty piles on their way to the Huntley power plant in western New York. There, other coughing men labored in coal dust and fly ash and dreamed that they were somewhere else. In the Huntley coal yard, where several hundred thousand tons were kept in constant reserve, the coal was gradually pushed to and fro to prevent it from erupting into flame under the pressure and heat of its own immense weight. The shifting mountain dwarfed the growling bulldozers as if they were Chihuahuas nipping at the heels of a sluggish giant. The men on the dozers coughed.

Sheets of black dust flowed down the slopes of the black mountain whenever it rained. Out onto the swirling Niagara River and fast past the downstream string of factories, refineries, mills, and waste sites between the rusty cities of Buffalo and Niagara Falls. To create the thousand-degree steam that spun its enormous turbines, Huntley each day guzzled nearly a billion gallons of the river and chewed up and burned seventy-five hundred tons of the shifting mountain without diminishing its lumpy black size. The long trains and trucks and lake freighters never ceased their full coming and empty going—like the workers who came and went through the gate house of the plant.

My father was one of them.

He began to work at Huntley in 1948, when Buffalo was still a major city. But both the city and the plant would age badly. By the 1960s, Huntley still provided electricity to over a million homes and hundreds of factories, but it had become creaky and cranky. In the intense heat and din of the laboring plant, most of the three hundred workers spent their shifts sweeping the thickly dusty floors, shoveling up the constantly spilling and leaking coal, and repairing the machinery. And dreaming of other places.

At the end of his long shift, my father showered away the fly ash and coal dust, changed into clean clothes, then drove to a bedroom community where the light was bright and the heat effortless. He entered his cozy house swinging his lunch pail and looking as scrubbed as when he had left for work. And as long as he did not cough up black phlegm or work up a gray sweat, no one in our bright and clean home would notice how much ash and dust had lodged in his lungs and pores. Not even my mother, who greeted him with a kiss full on the lips. Instead, his family sensed the plant's residual dirt and noise and heat in his weary being, taking note of his mounting agitation, like a team of weathermen trying to predict the arrival of a storm.

Dad went to work for the Niagara Mohawk Power Corporation right out of high school. He was assigned to work at Huntley in the utility crew.

The workers called it the shit crew.

Each morning the utility foreman swore over the phone at his gray metal desk while he received instructions from above, tipping back in his chair as he spoke. The crew of ten sat on battered wooden benches, heads bowed, eyes half-closed, yawning, moaning, muttering profanities. My father was usually ordered to sweep floors. Fresh sawdust soaked with oil in a wheelbarrow had to be scattered over the concrete, then piled by push broom into black heaps that were shoveled back into the wheelbarrow, three loads to every original one, then the whole lot shoveled into a Dumpster. By the next day the floor would again be coated with coal dust and fly ash. Sweeping was not particularly tiring, but on a hot summer day the top floor of the plant might reach 120 degrees. Filth clung to my father's sweat-drenched work suit and ground into his skin.

As much as he hated the monotonous sweeping, there were worse jobs. On one Monday the utility foreman slammed down his telephone receiver as the eight o'clock bell clamored, and asked a worker who had the same job each day, "Harry, what the fuck you waitin' for?" Next came the floor assignments: "Bob, Tony, Fred: sweep two, three, and four. Alex and John: seven and eight. Then get back to me. You hear, Alex?"

"Yeah."

"An' don't take all fuckin' day up there, either."

The foreman said to my father, "Same place as Friday, boy."

He was up and out without speaking. More than one hundred workers were on the day shift, but the plant was so immense that he encountered no one until he had crossed a cement corridor with grating and arrived at an elevator. Along with two mute men from maintenance, he entered the elevator, which already held eight other mute men. It rose through the piercing noise and intensifying heat, stopping several times before reaching a screaming floor. There he made his way past a huge pump that was making most of the noise; then he went along a narrow grated walkway between boilers and climbed up a ladder to a cramped four-foot-high area above a boiler.

Crouched on his hands and knees, he surveyed the space. Most of the area was deep in fly ash. A long hose, connected to the vacuum system of the plant, lay in fresh ash that had accumulated since Friday, when he had left much of the area clean. He put on goggles, then a respirator. Immediately his perspiring face felt uncomfortable within the rubber and he began the labored deep breathing necessary to obtain a sufficient air supply. He pushed off his cap and crawled farther in, and picked up the eight-inch-circumference vacuum hose. He handled it gently, but fly ash began to fill the air and adhere to his sweaty work suit and skin. A few minutes later, another member of the utility crew, with a shovel, joined him, and the air quickly became saturated as the two men, shoveling and vacuuming, worked blindly in a gray cloud.

After several months in utility, he was trained to weld and was promoted to the maintenance department, where his own father was foreman. There my father was as happy as when he had first been hired by the power company, and this time he didn't become as disappointed. He worked in the same noise and heat and dirt, and his ankles and feet and wrists were severely seared whenever molten metal splattered into his shoes or gloves. But now he was a skilled laborer and problem solver with job security and a fair paycheck. Now truly he was set for life.

He proposed marriage to Eva Wagner.

And as he perspired at his wedding reception, coal dust and fly ash flushed from his pores and turned his white shirt gray.

My grandfather climbed out of the Dodge on the slushy shoulder of the road, a cigarette dangling from his lips. My father speared the snow shovel into a lumpy pile. He searched his coat pockets for his pack, bumped the bottom on his wrist, removed the last cigarette with his lips, crumpled the pack, and dropped it back into the pocket. As my father lit up, his right hand holding the stainless steel lighter and his left hand cupped around the windward side of the cigarette, my grandfather, a little out of breath, asked, "Have you picked names yet?"

"Yep."

"Another Barley, huh?"

"We thought about it, but then we decided that if we name a boy after you, every time someone said, 'Barley, stop picking your nose,' neither of you could be sure which one they meant."

"Or, 'Barley, get out of that beer.' "

Dad took another drag and, exhaling, said, "Kim Arden if it's a girl, and Mark James if it's a boy."

Barley looked into the road where a car was slinging slush and shook his head twice. "Bad luck, that name James. Don't know how it got started in the family. There were James Phillipses even back in Ireland." He brushed snow off the back bumper of Dad's car, sat on it. My grandfather reminded Dad that Uncle James had died in a construction fall, and less than a year later one-year-old James Junior had died from pneumonia. "And in Ireland one of my father's brothers was a James who as a boy got his skull cracked with a hammer in a fight with one of his brothers. After that he never could read or write anymore. So as you can see, that name taunts fate."

My father well knew the family legends, but playing along, he asked, "Then why the hell did you name me James?"

"We couldn't give up hope, could we?"

Most of us know the American legends: the surnames and ethnic backgrounds and other details vary, but not the thrust of the stories. The Welsh horse-trading ancestor, whose first name is now forgotten, who settles in Ireland during the eighteenth century. The Welsh-Irish great-grandfather who runs away from the horse farm to work in the Belfast shipyards, and when work slows, he steams to America and becomes a successful blacksmith in booming Buffalo. The grandfather who becomes an ironworker even though two of his older brothers have fallen to death on the job—but who, after breaking two ribs on the job, takes a safer and better paying job as a power company foreman. The father who becomes a welder at the same plant. All of them always chasing work, capturing it, becoming better.

In these legends, equal opportunity laws don't exist, the wife stays home, the kids do their homework. Each generation buys a bigger house than did the one before, and the American economy grows stronger forever. Yet within the telling of these apple-pie legends comes a long pause. The forward march of material betterment halts, a gap like an erased portion of a tape recording, a story within a story untold. Occasionally it happens when the teller has just mentioned in passing, attempting nonchalance, the death of his father or mother. Suddenly weary, he rests. And before the momentum of the legends drives him forward again, he dreams of a small retirement farm on the lake plains or a hunting cabin in the Alleghenies—and only then, but often enough, will he tell a story of tragedy or disappointment.

It was from my father and uncles that I heard the legends, but never from the person who had passed the lengthening legends on to them—never from my grandfather. By the time I had turned eight in 1960, I was spending more time with him than with my overtime-working, tired, and easily irritated father, but I heard no legends from my grandfather. By then Grandpa had sold his home on bustling Pries Avenue in Buffalo and was living with Grandma in the countryside. Along with a small house, his rural property consisted of a chicken coop, cramped workshop, and vacant barn on eleven flat acres of abandoned crop land. The house had a leaky roof and drafty windows and peeling paint, as if he had traded his large and sturdy city home for one that better reflected his old age.

In the yard on warm summer evenings, sitting in metal lawn chairs or stretched out on the grass near the pear trees and hand-operated water pump and metal pink flamingos and free-ranging chickens stalking dew worms, Grandpa sipped beer and I gulped pop and we talked until dark. On spring mornings, we hiked the abandoned fields beyond the barn, where suddenly cock pheasants leapt, beating into cackling flight in the intense slanting sunlight—exploding prisms. In the cool barn, we shared seats on moldy bales of hay while among the rafters pigeons flapped and cooed and sparrows chirped and fluttered, and we could almost hear, in the faint wafting odors of old manure, the lowing of long-departed cattle. He gently teased me, encouraged me to talk about my life, listened sincerely.

But because I was too young to believe it, my grandfather never told me what he had learned in his old age about the impossibility of forever. And so together we drifted lazily over sunken family legends that I had yet to learn and he was trying to forget.

Once when he was preparing to smoke wasps out of his workshop, he pointed above the workbench to a large framed photograph of a man with thick frosty hair and bushy eyebrows, a long nose, a handlebar mustache, a stern expression. The man was his father. Although my grandfather didn't keep the photograph in the house, he hadn't discarded it; he kept it in the workshop, as if his memories of his father were inextricably tied to labor. After he identified the man, I asked why I didn't know him. He explained that his father was "long dead"—and then he fell quiet for a while before beginning to tell me about his dream of someday visiting Ireland and Wales.

The youngest of eight children, my father never knew his paternal grandfather except through the family legends that begin with the unnamed Welsh ancestor who settles in Ireland. The legends accelerate with the story of my father's grandfather, Samuel Phillips, running away from the Ulster farm and sailing to a new land. The legends are full of prideful work, and yet are gripped by the clutch of gravity, the power of molten rock—bettered lives nonetheless hurtling to earth. The laboring of the heroes cannot alter the endings. And sometimes, as in the tragic legend about the man my father was named after, labor is the ending.

The story always begins, "It was a cold morning in 1918."

It was a cold morning in 1918. After stepping onto a beam from a barge listing with a cargo of iron beams, James Phillips rode the ascending strip of iron. He gripped one of the spreaders of the cable, wrapped slowly upward by the chugging and popping cantilever crane. The beam swung slightly in the wind that gusted off the wide icy river. On days like that, with the metal cold and taut and stressed by the wind, he worried about joining his older brother, who a year earlier fell to his death—or, as ironworkers describe such accidents, "took the dive." One part of him feared, and a different part of him reasoned that it couldn't happen twice to the same family.

He puffed on the stub of a cigarette hanging from his lips and gazed out over the moving ice and shivered in the moist wind. When the beam was so high that he could see the white earth curve far beyond the opposite shoreline, wind rushed through the open skeleton of the bridge with sounds like random organ notes blasting crazily. He noticed that the cable was gradually twisting, and he crouched and cursed the part of himself that made him choose to ride the beam rather than the elevator cage. The beam had nearly reached its destination, where three of his buddies waited, yelling down to him words that he couldn't make out in the wind, when he heard a sharp bang. He knew that no automobile, nor the crane engine, had backfired;

he understood, even in the split second before he was in midair, that the cable had snapped.

I heard it more often than I heard any of the others—a half dozen times before I turned nine years old—"The Story of the James Phillips Who Fell."

The tale of work, gravity, the reclaiming earth.

One morning my grandmother told my grandfather a shocking story about himself. Dad was sipping tea and reading the Sunday *Courier-Express* and smoking cigarettes. Several butts were heaped in the clear glass ashtray in the middle of the kitchen table. Mom was washing the breakfast dishes, and I was sitting across from Dad, trying to gulp down my cereal and milk before he recalled or noticed something that I had done wrong. Grandpa strode into our house without knocking and abruptly stopped in the middle of the kitchen. "This morning your ma doesn't know who I am. She doesn't know me. When I told her, she said her husband is dead."

Dad said, "She said that?"

"Yes. I'm dead."

"She's not there alone, is she?"

"No. Your sister—"

He broke down.

Mom led me up to my room. I asked her why Grandpa was crying, and she tried to explain, but I couldn't understand. Hadn't Grandma always been old and blind and funny in the head?

Even after she lost her eyesight, my grandmother had managed to cook, feeling her way around the kitchen. But I always took it for granted that even blind women should cook for their husbands. I was far more impressed by her ability to find her way to the television set, switch it on, and settle back into the rocking chair whenever the clock chimes told her that Groucho Marx would be cracking jokes on *You Bet Your Life.*

Grandpa once left me with her when he went out to feed the chickens and collect eggs. I tried to sneak hard candy from the glass bowl on the coffee table. But somehow she heard as I carefully lifted the lid, and asked sweetly, "Mark, why don't you have a piece of candy?" Convinced she was faking her blindness, I walked up to the rocking chair and waved my hands in front of her eyes. She didn't flinch.

Although blindness didn't confuse her, hardening of the arteries did. Sometimes she insisted Grandpa was still an ironworker helping to build a bridge over the Niagara River and that they still lived on Pries Avenue in Buffalo. During her spells Grandpa had to be with her constantly; otherwise, she might leave a pot of food burning on the stove while she wandered down the cellar stairs to change the diaper of an imaginary newborn in a nonexistent nursery.

Until that day when he wept in our kitchen, Grandpa often spoke to my father about wanting to visit Ireland and Wales. He had wanted to meet his cousins who still lived on the small stony farm that had been his grandfather's; wanted to walk the walled boundaries of the land, enter the dank dimness of the barn, touch the cool thick walls of the white cottage; wanted to visit the grave of the grandfather he'd never met, in the stony land of Ulster, unmarked. Wanted to bring home a jar filled with soil of Wales, the place of origin; another with soil of Ireland, the place of interlude; and a third filled with the merging water of the Atlantic.

But then Grandma told him, as if he were already a ghost, that her husband was dead. He never again mentioned Ireland or Wales.

Several weeks after that morning in 1961 when Grandma informed Grandpa that he was dead, he fell ill. My family visited and found him laboring for air in his small bedroom, which was acrid with Vicks VapoRub and hot and sticky with vaporizer mist. He didn't seem to know I was present. Not understanding how weak he was with pneumonia—that he was slowly drowning—I felt slighted. I pushed aside the drape that served as a door and fled the crowded uncomfortable bedroom, striding past Grandma, who was rocking blindly in the small dim living room. And without putting on my coat, I stepped out into the cool air and sunshine of the open yard. On the bright thin fading snow, the red and white chickens clucked and scratched for food.

A few mornings after the disappointing visit, my mother sat on the edge of my bed and gently rubbed my back. As I woke, she told me I didn't have to go to school that day. My eyes popped wide and I asked, "How deep is the snow?"

She took a deep breath. "Grandpa Phillips has gone to heaven to live."

I sat up. "What do you mean?"

She said he had gone to heaven and would never be back. I still didn't understand. She explained that he had died in a hospital, and angels had taken his soul to heaven, and I would never see or talk to him again until some day a long time away when angels would also take my soul to heaven. I said, "No!" I lay back down and pressed my face into the pillow. And for the rest of the morning, I refused to talk to her.

I returned to school the day after the funeral. I told my friends that my grandfather had "died of ammonia." During the bus ride home, I walked up to Johnny Burbidge, a neighborhood playmate who was standing at the front of the bus. As the doors hissed open to let him out into his yard, I demanded to know, "You're glad my grandpa died; aren't you?" I wanted him to say he was glad, wanted an excuse to pretend he was one of the angels who had taken Grandpa to heaven. I desired to thrash him until he cried for his mother.

He looked at me curiously. "No, I'm not glad."

When I walked into my home, Mom asked how my day had gone. I shrugged. I climbed the stairway to my bedroom, shut the door, and crawled into bed. And I didn't leave my bedroom until late that evening when my father came home from working overtime at the plant.

That spring, Dad was working long hours of overtime while his brothers were putting in equally long hours as construction workers. Although all Grandma's children agreed to take turns caring for her, only my uncle Al took time off from his job to prepare the estate for sale. But he did not do so happily. He set aside some items: a few power tools, a double-barrel shotgun, a cookie jar, a set of green mugs from which his father and grandfather had sipped beer, the big family Bible, a box of curled photographs, a tattered feed bag full of freshly plucked and gutted poultry. Then, without checking with his absent siblings, he

trucked almost everything else to the nearest dump. The or-
nately framed photograph of his grandfather he left hanging in
the dusty workshop to greet the next owner.

By the time my father had a day off, it was too late. Floor-
boards creaking, he wandered the vacant house. He opened
closets, drawers, cupboards, all empty. Before he left each room
he paused to gaze around for a final time. I followed him, asking questions that he ignored. Where was everything and who
would live here and could this be a haunted house now and
who would feed the chickens and could we please please please
take them home with us and why was there an echo?

After he climbed down from the empty attic, we went outside and he locked up the house. The overwintered lawn was
beginning to grow again, and we could hear a raucous flock of
crows in the field beyond the barn. I followed him to the barn,
where he merely peered into the dimness and then over my ob-
jection passed by the chicken coop. When he opened the door to
the workshop we could hear the dull rattling buzz of wasps and
could see that still hanging on the wall above the workbench
was the framed photograph of his grandfather draped in cob-
webs. Dad quickly stepped to the bench as if he might take the
photo, but then merely stood there for a few moments before
turning to leave.

During the short drive home across Pendleton, we passed
the small ranch-style homes of factory workers where kids I recognized were playing quarrelsome basketball on concrete or
blacktopped driveways in the sudden heat, shirts and skins.
The road shimmering, we passed the flat treeless stretches of
farmland, some abandoned and weedy, and some recently
plowed, the dark soil clumped and warming in the sun. By then

I had given up asking questions, and while I gazed out the passenger-side window my father suddenly looked over at me as if he had just then realized I was along. "Well, Mark, whataya say? I guess you and me better go fishing. Don't you think?"

Because he had never taken me along on one of his fishing trips, I didn't know what to say except, "There's fish in one of the ponds behind the house."

He laughed. "No. Real fish, not stunted bullheads. We'll be after big fish. In the river or someplace like that."

"Today?"

"No, not today. Soon."

"How big will the fish be, Dad?"

"You know what else? This summer we're gonna go on a vacation, too."

"You mean summer vacation?"

"No. That's just being off school. I mean I'm gonna take time off work and we're gonna go on a real vacation."

"Johnny's family went on vacation last summer. Why do people go on vacation?"

"You'll see."

When we were home, he spread maps of New York and Ontario on the kitchen table. When Mom asked him where he was going, he replied, "I don't know where, but this summer we're all going on a vacation."

She asked, "Are you telling me a story?"

By the time my mother woke me on school mornings, she had cooked breakfast and laid out clothing for my sister and me and had filled the kitchen sink with steaming sudsy water; by the

time I was ready for school, the washing machine in the basement was already chugging. She kissed Kim and me as we left
the house, had milk and a snack on the kitchen table when we
returned from school, served a big homemade dinner, helped us
with our homework, tucked us in, and kissed us good night. We
were traveling through life in familiar territory. But one evening
she responded to Dad's criticism of a meal by overturning the
kitchen table—a different and rare sign that I didn't yet know
how to read.

Once while she was urging me to do better in school so that
someday I could go to college, I asked her if she had gone. She
looked up from her housework, laughed briefly, and said, "Back
then college was only for rich girls who wanted to find richer
husbands."

My mother had been valedictorian of her high school class,
but in our neighborhood in Pendleton in the 1960s, where the
women's liberation movement was merely a rumor, her intelli-
gence didn't matter. Few of the women worked outside the
home and even fewer had college educations. From early each
morning until late each evening, they cleaned, cooked, raised
children, and occasionally talked by telephone, the neighborhood grapevine through which it seemed the worst thing that
could be said about another woman was that her house was
dirty. Still, Mom did once take an entrance test offered by a cor-
respondence school for writers and was told she had "excellent
potential," a judgment that the grader probably would have
passed on Bonzo the Chimp. But despite Dad's halfhearted encouragement, or because of it, she decided against enrolling in
the school.

It was a few weeks after Mom decided against correspon-
dence school that she overturned the kitchen table. Later that
night, my sister and I woke to shouting. We children crept to the
edge of the stairs and listened in terror to bursts of words that
made no sense to us until Dad threatened to move out. We
rushed down the stairs, pleading, "Please don't go, Daddy!
Please!" Then our mother and father, at first shamefully and
then lovingly, embraced.

After he had settled into his chair and downed a few beers
the next evening, I asked Dad if he might still move out. At first
he shot me one of his fiery goddamnit-I'm-tired glares, but then
he noticed how frightened I was and quickly patted me on the
head, his sudden anger melting. "No, don't worry," he said.
"Parents just get in fights once in a while. All parents do. It
blows over." When he saw that I was still worried, he said, "The
guys at the plant who aren't married are miserable. Getting
married is the best thing I ever did." He added that Mom was a
damn good wife. "She's gotten better, too, the longer we've
been married. Having kids makes a woman better, just like having puppies makes a dog better."

A few weeks after the nighttime argument, Mom signed out of
the library several books about unidentified flying objects.
Every few days she finished one of the books and passed it on to
Dad, who for two weeks watched almost no television. To my
sister Kim and me they repeated harrowing stories about earth-
lings kidnapped by little green vivisectionists and about airplanes that crashed mysteriously or simply disappeared after
the pilots reported seeing strange metallic objects in the sky.

Soon, night after night, all four of us were spotting UFOs. Within a half mile of our house there was a much-used landing strip for small airplanes, but we chose to believe that the lights we were seeing were the "multicolored, hovering lights of alien spacecraft."

Then one day, without offering an explanation to the rest of us, Mom stopped reading and talking about UFOs. For the next several days, she cleaned and scrubbed with fury, as if she had suddenly looked up from a book and realized with panic that the real threat was within the house.

One afternoon while she was vacuuming the carpet beneath the coffee table, the sucking hum deepened and then rose into a high whine, the cleaner shaking, the odor of smoldering rubber, of a slipping belt, filling the house. She switched off the cleaner and tipped it on its side. Soon she extracted a plastic soldier. I thought she would complain about my having left it on the floor, but she didn't seem to notice me watching from the kitchen. She put the toy into her apron pocket, turned the machine right side up, switched it back on, waited a moment to be sure it was working properly, smiled, and patted the handle.

Over a month passed before we went fishing. The welding crew needed to work long weeks to help repair the machinery that frequently broke down in the old hulking plant. "You can't pick and choose your overtime," Dad often complained. "You start turning them down too much and they don't ask you anymore. They ask someone they know will always say yes."

He rarely had to work on Sundays, but often worked ten-hour shifts on weekdays and eight hours or more on Saturdays. During his time off he was exhausted. On a normal Sunday he slept until almost noon, ate the big fried breakfast that Mom had prepared, watched a football or baseball game if one was on television, then mowed the lawn or puttered at his workbench in the cellar. After that he gulped supper, watched more television, and drank beer. Around midnight, he shuffled off to bed or simply fell asleep in his easy chair. Then it was Monday again and my mother was saying, "Come on, Jim, wake up. Jim! You gotta go to work. Jim!"

Part of me was sorry to see him when he rose late on Sundays, and was glad to see him leave for work on Mondays. He labored in intense noise and filth and heat, welding inside boilers or crevasses of machinery, where the sparks and molten metal seared his skin and the acrid fumes inflamed his lungs. He might work under such conditions for sixty hours a week. I spent Sundays trying to avoid his glare; it was as if the welding arc had ignited something deep within him that made his stare hot. I sometimes could feel his glare burning the back of my head, and when I spun around I knew that I was about to be chewed out for having a messy room or mediocre grades in school or acting goofy with my friends. Or for avoiding him. If I didn't feel the heat fast enough, didn't spin soon enough, he might slap the back of my head. Other times, he said nothing, just glared, a hot silent treatment that might last for days.

His long silences should have relieved me: they meant that I wouldn't be yelled at or slapped. Instead they terrified me; I didn't want to lose him entirely. He was two men. One was tired

and irritated and explosive; the other, who was patient and re-
spectful, hadn't been working overtime or had just returned
from a fishing or hunting trip. When he was giving me the silent
treatment, I felt that I was losing both fathers.

One Sunday he rose early enough to take me fishing, and to set
the Erie Canal on fire. Literally. He slept in later than he had
planned, but we were at the dock by midmorning. While
gassing up the outboard motor, he spilled fuel onto the oily
water of the canal. When he dropped his cigarette, the floating
gasoline ignited and then the floating oil. The flames whooshed
fifty feet before he could scramble back onto the dock, but just
as suddenly as it had started, the fire extinguished. Shaking his
head, he muttered, "Son of a bitch. Son of a bitch." He sat down
on the edge of the dock, his feet dangling over the water, and
watched the black smoke lift and dissipate. He said, "I need a
Genny."

He walked to the car, opened the trunk, and lifted out a
brown bottle of Genesee beer. As he returned to the dock with
the bottle and chest, I suddenly recovered my ability to speak.
"The water caught on fire!" I yelled, pointing. "The water
caught on fire!" Dad opened the bottle, tossed the top into the
canal, and gulped, his head tipping back until his red cap fell to
the dock.

Eventually we departed, the bluish exhaust of the twenty-
horse motor hanging in the air behind our little rented boat. The
boat was continually rocked by the wakes of bigger boats in the
narrow canal. We passed under painted steel bridges and by
floating tree branches, plastic bottles, dead fish, turds, brown
and white foam, past a field where small boys threw rocks that

fell short of us, past backyards where people waved from lawn chairs.

While we passed a cemetery, Dad told me that the canal was lined with the graves of the men who had dug it. Irish immigrants who "were called canawlers and died like flies and were replaced with new canawlers who died just as fast." They worked with picks, shovels, and dynamite, inching through muck and clay and bedrock for a monthly payment of ten dollars, board, and several jiggers of whiskey. Each summer for many years, he said, the completed canal was briefly drained and the canawlers hurriedly cleaned it of silt, trash, sunken logs, rotting corpses.

And then once again he was telling me "The Story of the James Phillips Who Fell."

When eventually we chugged into the Niagara River, I felt that the entire breathtaking world had unfolded into wide sparkling blue. I saw zooming pleasure boats and a tug pulling a barge and a distant freighter that Dad said might be loaded with coal for the power plant, and beyond the boats the shoreline of Canada, the aluminum window panes and white siding of houses flashing in the bright sunshine. Sitting on the backseat, Dad swung the motor, aimed the boat upstream, and opened the throttle; the engine sputtered and then roared and belched smoke, and the propeller churned up heaps of water, slowly moving the boat against the current that ran strong to the falls.

It was almost noon and hot despite the breeze when he cut the motor. We were offshore from a red brick building that was longer than a football field and rose several stories in a jumble of variously shaped and sized tiers. "Well, this is where I work."

On the hot aluminum seat I slid to the side of the boat near-est the shore and stared at the plant. Dad's job was so much a part of our family conversation and so shaped our lives that the words "the plant" always registered like the name of a boss, as if my father or mother were talking about someone powerful who was named Mr. Plant. Now from my seat in the boat, I saw that the closer a brick tier was to the river, the squatter it was, as if Mr. Plant were crouched forward to drink. The river swirled where water was guzzled in and passed out through the im-mense submerged pipes. The humming of the jumbled trans-formers rose and fell, like troubled breathing. Long trucks were lined up in the coal yard, dumping black food near the mechan-ical feeders; other long trucks were carrying away what my fa-ther told me was fly ash, the waste matter. Mr. Plant belched steamy heat and ireful smoke into the sky. I tried to see what was in the belly of the big boss, but the windows were too grimy. Pointing up at a catwalk that ringed the top of a towering smoke stack, I thought of "The Story of the James Phillips Who Fell." I asked, "Do you ever have to weld way up there?"

"Not very often."

We dropped anchor. He told me that whenever workers cleaned the water intake screens of the plant, they discovered that scores of big fish had been trapped by the powerful suck-ing. A worker once hooked onto something so heavy that a buddy had to help him raise the long cleaning rake, hand over hand, until an enormous sturgeon flopped bleeding on the floor of the Water Intake Building. They preserved the sturgeon on a wheelbarrow loaded with cafeteria ice. That evening they sold their catch, laden with roe, to a seafood shop for one hundred dollars—about a dollar for each year that the fish had lived.

We baited our hooks with live crawfish. Sweating in the sun's glare, talking, eating sandwiches and candy, drinking beer or pop, pissing into the water, daydreaming, we fished for two hours without a nibble. Then the line suddenly stripped off my reel, the drag buzzing. But before I could react the line went limp—broken. "Jesus Christ!" said Dad. "That was a hell of a fish! A muskie, I'll bet ya anything!"

For a while, we leaned forward with our eyes fixed on the narrow tips of our rods, expecting another huge fish to seize one of our hooked crawfish. But the water swept by the anchored boat, and the sun crept brightly, and we became bored with the gently bobbing ends of our fiberglass rods, watching instead the water skiers out on the blue river beneath the blue sky as we sweated in the aluminum boat. Once we were rocked by the wake of a long fiberglass speedboat, its pointy bow bouncing above the water as it roared close to our little craft. Dad became surly. "One of the big bosses at the plant has a boat like that," he said. "You'll never see him working on a weekend. If he fishes, I'll bet he hires somebody to clean them."

He had been yawning all morning, and now, with his reddened tired eyes, he glared back at the power plant, its sooty darkness, and ignored my questions. Eventually, he said, "I don't know why the hell I picked this spot. I guess I'm too used to coming here for work."

I felt the welding arc as he fixed his eyes on me. I knew that the plant had reclaimed one of my fathers, and had left me in the little boat with the other. But I didn't want our day together to end yet. I failed to heed the heat. "Let's move," I said. "Let's try a different spot."

"Ah, the hell with it. They're not biting. And I'm tired. We're going home."

"But Dad—we haven't caught anything."

Suddenly he was more than surly. "Don't you appreciate anything?" he shouted. "I finally get a day off and we went fishing. Do you know how tired I am? Do you know what it cost me to rent this boat?"

"Okay, Dad. It's okay."

He glared at me for another moment. Then as he turned away, I felt the electricity in his eyes flicker and nearly go out. He quietly asked, "We had a good time—didn't we?"

All the way back, I thought about the fish that had gotten away. Dad believed it had been a muskellunge, but I was sure it had been a sturgeon. I still daydream about it: an immense sturgeon finning slowly over the bottom of the mighty Niagara, my rusty childhood hook yet embedded in its prehistoric mouth.

Like the other men who worked at the power plant, my father endured by dreaming. When a man felt his consciousness sweating away in the heat or was deafened by the rattling thunder of coal or had a coughing spell that left his sleeve smeared with black mucus, he turned inward and pictured, beyond work, a soothing shower and a delicious home-cooked meal and a soft easy chair and numbing beer and fantastical television and cool clean sheets. But then he also saw another day and week and month and year and decade and decade and decade at the plant. And so he dreamed.

Surely some of the men dreamed of striking it rich. Or of a younger and prettier and hornier wife with a flatter stomach and firmer breasts. Or of violence: the old lady bleeding from her bitching mouth, the neck of the girlfriend's husband cut from ear to ear, the nosy neighbor's ass kicked, the fucking power plant blown to Kingdom Come. But just as surely, most of the men dreamed of simple and peaceful pleasures. Dreamt of the house finally paid off and of shiny new linoleum for the kitchen, and of kids, of smiling kids and their smiling mother who would gratefully scrub the new linoleum. Or dreamt of a boat out on the blue breezy river, or of a cozy cottage or cabin where the door opened to clean air and a view of the glassy lake or green mountains far from the power plant. Work was the price of pleasure. Boring dangerous filthy sweaty deafening work bought relief from itself.

Dad had long dreamt of buying land and building a cabin, but since Grandpa's death he had also been dreaming of a third child. In his dream he must have seen himself entering his house with his empty lunch pail, the rattling of coal still echoing in his head as a baby crawled to him across the new linoleum with a squeal. The echoes would fade and he would grin and reach down and swing the baby high, as light as a dream, and he would say to his wife, who stood smiling beatifically in the sparkling kitchen where she never tired or aged, "Good news! I don't have to work this weekend! We can all go to the cabin!"

Mom had a simpler dream. She wanted the new linoleum.

Mom knew where his dreams would leave her: home with morning sickness and a fat belly and swollen ankles, then diapers to change while he worked overtime to pay the new bills. Or home doing yet more cooking and dishes and ironing while he spent his weekends building his dream cabin. Or the whole family would take a vacation at the dream cabin where she would do the cooking and cleaning and diaper changing.

While growing up, I heard my parents fight openly on merely three or four occasions, but for several weeks their opposing dreams quietly clashed. Although I didn't understand its cause until years later when my mother explained it to me, I could feel the tension in the house. Her hugs and kisses were quicker than usual when he came home from the plant, as if she were afraid where the greetings might lead, and she made frequent mention of how much housework she had to do. Our meals became blander and smaller and I could see my father fighting back his anger as he ate. Once at the dinner table she broke the uncomfortable quiet by saying, "Wouldn't you kids like new bedrooms? If I had a job, maybe we could have a whole new house."

With prompt alarm I made it clear that I didn't want a new house, and asked who would take care of me if she took a job.

She pretended she hadn't heard.

And when she wasn't looking, he winked at me.

Each year my father took one of his two weeks of vacation to make home improvements. In the summer of 1958, so that Kim and I no longer would have to share a bedroom, Dad converted our small living room into a bedroom and started building a new and bigger living room. In 1959, he finished the living room and poured a sidewalk. In 1960, he replaced the shingles and put down new linoleum in the bathroom. But in 1961, several weeks after setting the canal on fire, he announced, "I don't care if this place falls down, this family is gonna go on vacation just like I promised."

With several suitcases and boxes of food packed in the Ford, we rode to Chautauqua Lake, eighty miles southwest of Buffalo, where Dad had rented a small cottage and a boat with a powerful motor. There my parents forgot about bills and babies and his job, and they teased and tickled each other and had pillow fights that my sister Kim and I joined. And each afternoon all of us rode to the middle of the lake, where Dad or Mom jumped into the water and pulled on skis. Then the other parent opened the throttle slightly, and the rope gradually tightened, the motor briefly sputtering and smoking before it roared, and the skier rose onto the lake, weaving, bouncing over the wakes, arms outstretched as if reaching—but we were too far ahead, we kids, to be caught.

On the final morning of our vacation, Dad and I went fishing. He anchored the boat where the owner of a bait shop had suggested. In two hours we caught only a few small perch. Then Dad took off his shirt and sandals and in his shorts dove from the boat, staying down for so long that I feared he would never come up. As I leaned far over the side of the boat, staring desperately into the darkening green, he popped up gasping and grinning on the opposite side, waving triumphantly in his right hand a small white rock that dripped and glistened in the sunlight.

While we were returning to the cottage, we noticed that a fisherman in another boat had hooked something powerful: his pole was bent nearly double. His companion, who held a net, motioned for us to approach. When we were close to the other boat Dad cut our motor, and the man with the net yelled, "Do you have a gaff hook?" Dad shook his head, and the man yelled, "Damn!" The man looked around wildly as if a gaff hook might magically materialize, then yelled, "He's got a helluva muskie on! We got a net but he's too big! He's a big one! We need a gaff hook!" The man who was battling the fish didn't speak. His hair and shirt were soaked with sweat. Straining, he repeatedly lifted and lowered his rod, rapidly reeling in the slack. But each time he had the fish near the boat and his companion tried to net it, the water erupted and line stripped off the reel as the fish made another diving run.

Eventually the exhausted muskellunge seemed to give up. Almost five feet long, it surfaced on its side close to the boat, pink gills opening and closing, green and silver scales glittering in the sun. The netter slipped as much of the netting as he could over the fish and lifted. But when the fish was almost into the boat it thrashed, and the man dropped the net and fish into the water and the fish shook its big head splashing both men, and the red and white spoon with treble hooks was flung loose and the muskellunge was gone. The netter bent over at the waist each time he screamed it: "Fuck! Fuck! Fuck! Fuck! Fuck!"

The other man sat down without speaking, still clutching the pole, dripping and gasping like a fish out of water.

On the Monday morning following our vacation, my father said even less than usual as he readied for work. At the kitchen table he chain-smoked and stirred his tea furiously, the spoon loudly clanging the ceramic cup, tea spilling on the Formica tabletop. I gulped my cereal so that I could soon flee the table. I saw it on his face: Fuck! Fuck! Fuck! Fuck! Fuck!

A control-room operator made a mistake, and the electronic signal closed the boiler door before Dad was out with the last of his tools and equipment. He stood there for a moment in the sudden darkness, then began feeling around for the utility light before recalling that he'd already taken it out. Now he couldn't even find the door. While lurching around in the dark, he banged his head on something hard and almost lost consciousness. As he recovered on his hands and knees, he remembered the Zippo cigarette lighter in his pocket.

The small flame of the lighter reminded him that someone intended to start up the boiler. With the lid flipped back he set the lighter on the floor and saw the door, and in the faint shifting light and shadows of the yellow and blue flame he thought: I'm going to be burned alive. He screamed for help. He fought the thick steel door. After his throbbing hands began to bleed, he threw his shoulder against the steel and kicked at it as the small flame flickered out. Then he crawled around feeling for the lighter. Instead of the lighter, he found one of his welding clamps, and crawled back to the door to bang on it with the clamp as he hollered in darkness. His arms became heavy and his voice hoarse, and every few seconds he had to stop, chest heaving. While he rested, he listened for the sound of pulverized coal moving through the chutes above the boiler. He heard the rasping of his lungs.

A maintenance worker, on his way to retrieve a wrench, heard the weakening pounding and faint cries. He ran to the phone on the far wall and dialed and said, "You goddamn fools got a man trapped in a boiler."

Dad always referred to the control room as "the cloud room" because it was clean and air-conditioned and some of the engineers and operators wore white shirts—and now, a fugitive from hell, he knelt on the blackened concrete floor outside the boiler to catch his breath before charging fire-breathing into the clouds.

It must have been hard for her to say no to her husband who had almost become fuel for a boiler that produced steam to turn the turbines that generated the electricity that lit our home. They must have slid between the sheets and held each other for a long time.

They must have turned out the lights.

It was my first time in a restaurant. I was wearing my Sunday clothes and a clip-on bow tie that pinched the skin of my neck, and had been instructed by my parents to talk quietly and to use my very best manners and to spread the cloth napkin on my lap when the food came. Dad had taken the day off and seemed as rested and relaxed as when our family had taken its lakeside vacation.

"When will we eat?" Kim and I kept asking.

"Soon," our parents kept promising.

The meal was worth the long wait. Charbroiled steak was even better than grilled hot dogs. And while we all ate a dessert of cheesecake, which was almost as delicious as Mom's chocolate chip cookies, she announced to Kim and me that in five months we would be getting a new brother or sister.

This was turning out to be a great day. Steak, cheesecake, and now a new pet.

"Shhhhh! Calm down," she said. "Keep your voices down."

The older couple at the next table had shot us a look. I wanted to ask my parents what was wrong with the lady's face; her mouth wasn't shaped quite right and the taut skin of her cheeks didn't match her wrinkled neck wrapped in pearls. But I was afraid of another one of those looks that would make me feel small and smelly. The couple didn't want us to make noise, but they were making plenty of noise themselves. They didn't like their meals. They kept complaining to the waitress that the meat was done too much or not enough or something didn't taste right and there was a spot on the tablecloth and it was taking too long to get their coffee refilled and there wasn't enough sour cream for the baked potato or soft enough butter for the rolls. The waitress with varicose veins hurried back and forth between their table and the kitchen and never argued. When she was busy elsewhere they went on complaining to each other. The man ate all of his meal and the lady left only a morsel of steak and a spoonful of applesauce. They ordered dessert.

When the waitress brought the check to the people who weren't from Pendleton, my father stood up and said, "Here's the tip for those people. I don't think they can afford it."

By the time we were almost home, Kim had fallen asleep curled up on the backseat. As we glanced through the passing picture windows at the people watching television, music played low on the car radio and the tires hummed over Bear Ridge Road and my mother's head rested against my father's shoulder as he sang along with Sinatra and drove us to our home that would seem new again.

In November Dad took his second week of vacation to go deer hunting in the hills south of Buffalo. Each morning he was in the car by five, and in the woods of Allegany State Park by daybreak. He hunted until dark, ate a big greasy meal at a diner, and was back home by nine. He kept that up until he was too exhausted to get out of bed on Friday morning.

When he finally got out of bed on Friday afternoon, his sixth-straight day off work, he was rested and relaxed. By the time he was back from the park each night, we kids were in bed, so he hadn't seen us all week; but on Friday afternoon he came out to help Kim and me build a carrot-nosed snowman in the front yard.

I asked him if he would take me with him on Saturday.

Anyone who knows anything about deer knows they have excellent eyesight and hearing, and anyone who knows anything about nine-year-old boys knows they have trouble holding still and staying quiet. Yet Dad replied, "Yes, of course."

In the car on Saturday morning he gave me a blanket and pillow and told me to go back to sleep. But the dark world beyond midnight was to me a new continent. The houses were shadowy mysteries until briefly illuminated by our car lights. There were no other cars on the road and the occasional truck seemed exotic, the red taillights like the beady fiery eyes of a great beast of the night. I searched the starry sky in vain for the moon. I asked questions about our drive and destination and deer hunting until Dad sharply ordered me to go to sleep. In the backseat I pulled a blanket over me, the insulated clothing and freshly oiled shotgun on the humped floor in front of me, the radio murmuring, the studded snow tires loudly vibrating over the pavement, the pillow cool, the back of my father's head risen into the sky ahead.

I didn't wake until he pulled the car off a back road in the park. Two other cars were parked ahead of us, and in the dim interior light of one I could see three men moving around. For a moment I didn't know where I was. Then Dad reached back for his hunting coat and gun, and suddenly I was wide awake, pulling on the layers of warm and bright clothing Mom had packed.

In the cold predawn, we urinated on the gravelly shoulder of the road. I thought it was already dawn until I followed Dad into the forest where, despite the gray sky and murky snow squeaking beneath my insulated rubber boots, I could see only the nearest of trees. The terrain was so steep and I was following so near that I repeatedly stepped on the back of his boots until he took my hand and had me walk at his side as we descended the slippery hillside.

By the time we reached his hunting spot, I could see well enough to know I was far deeper into a forest than ever before. The dense stand of hemlock behind us was yet in darkness, but ahead of us I could see stark hardwoods on rough land gradually descending to a small rocky stream. On the far side of the stream, the land rose out of dimness until leveling far above us, where a long tangled windfall of timber was lit by an expanding fringe of sunlight. Birds fluttered off their roosts in the hemlocks while Dad explained to me in a whisper that when other hunters pressured the deer they sometimes escaped through the valley and up into the cover of the hemlock. He sat down with his back against a wide tree and told me to sit with my back against the other side and, once again, reminded me to stay very still and quiet.

I listened to the stream and the first jays and chickadees. When it was lighter, I removed the rolled comic books from my coat pocket and began to read, following Dad's plan to keep me occupied. I jumped a little each time a gunshot echoed through the hills and was glad when the sun was above the hemlocks and bathing me in rays because by then I was shivering. I tried to stay still and quiet but I laughed aloud when Veronica pushed Jughead into a swimming pool. As the morning wore on I had to move my legs when they kept falling asleep and was plagued by itches that intensified and multiplied although I tried to ignore them. And every half hour or so, I felt I had to stand and pee.

At about ten o'clock, Dad sighed and said we might as well walk around. He told me to step only in his tracks. Although he walked very slowly and kept stopping to look around, I found it hard to concentrate and kept forgetting to step in his tracks instead of on the snow-covered branches that cracked. At around noon he led me out of the forest along a brushy sunny ravine cut by a stream. On the snowy bank of the stream we sat down to eat our packed lunches.

While we ate, he told me about earlier hunts in the park when he had seen a bear and a bobcat, about having tracked an old buck with strange backswept horns like a billy goat's until he had surprised it in its bed and had shot it as it had crested a mountain. Then he said, "You know, Mark, what we need is a cabin and some land of our own. You'd be okay in a cabin while I was out hunting, wouldn't you?"

"I like going with you best."

"I see."

I asked if I could play in the stream. He thought for a moment, then said okay. I clambered backward down the steep bank. The swift flow was clear and shallow, and for a long while I turned up slippery rocks and tried to catch crawfish. Then I built a dam, pilling up flat rocks and stuffing the cracks with moss and dead leaves. I sailed sticks in my little reservoir, battleships, and launched stones at them. When eventually I happened to pick up a crumbly stone laced with shells—fossilized before the Alleghenies had risen from the sea—I scrambled up the bank, my pants soaked and hands red and water sloshing inside my boots, to show my father. And I found him stretched out on his back with his bright woolen hunting coat balled up beneath his head, on the snow, in the sun asleep.

April was born in May. She came home with a scab on the tip of her nose where she'd rubbed the skin raw on the mattress of a hospital crib. My maternal grandfather, who was a farmer, laughed when he saw her. "I know what she was looking for! Hungry! Rooting around for titty like a pig in the sod."

Dad took two personal days to stay home and help, but all manner of relatives and neighbors visited, and neither Mom nor the baby got much rest. In the crowded kitchen, the women oohed and ahhed and reached for the baby. In the stratified smoke of the living room, the joking men slapped Dad on the back and lit up cigars and drank beer and whiskey and ate sandwiches and watched a ball game on television. My Uncle Al and Aunt Doris brought Grandma Phillips, whose blind eyes sparkled as April was placed gently in her arms.

By the second evening, Mom could no longer stay awake. Dad cooked our supper while Mom slept. Kim and I took turns holding April, who cried whenever she was set down, a sound like the baaing of a sheep. She didn't want her bottle and kept baaing as I patted her back and walked around the house with her bundled in my arms. From the stove, Dad said, "Talk to her."

"Talk?"

"Sure. In a nice voice. And quiet. Just talk."

"About what?"

He smiled. "It doesn't matter. She doesn't understand. Just do it in a nice quiet voice. I dunno. Tell her a story."

"A story?"

"Is there an echo in here? Yes, a story."

I thought for a few moments before I began in my sweetest voice: "It was a cold morning in 1918."

⮞◆⮜

As they finish constructing the lean-to of stout beech and maple saplings and wide sheets of elm bark, Horace Guild says, We haven't made one of these since we were kids, and David Hibner replies, Now it ain't play, and Horace nods gravely. Then they unstrap the packs from the horses and pile them within the lean-to. Pausing only to drink on their hands and knees from the cold murmuring spring, they begin to select and cut trees. Felling hardwoods is difficult and slow work, but no conifers or poplar grow nearby, and the young men swing their axes with the knowledge that soon they will be bringing their wives and children to make a new life on land that is more thin and stony than the land agent said when convincing them to choose on credit a dream from a new map of ancient wilderness.

Not until the forest is fast darkening do they put down their axes. They build a fire that is too large for comfort, then Horace slides the jug of spirits from a pack and the two men begin to pass it back and forth. They sit perspiring before the fire and look out at the dim pile of logs for the first of the two cabins. They congratulate themselves heartily and share the jug some more, then cook their meals too quickly, eat even the sooty parts ravishingly, and drink more spirits while talking of their families and friends back home. Eventually they add to the fire more dead wood and a thick log of green maple and take final swigs from the jug before stretching out on blankets alongside their muskets, talking about home.

Staring past the flames and into the darkness, they tell each other it is probably just the horses moving around out there. Then for a long while neither speaks.

Horace stares and listens and wonders. He begins to think about the long howling winter only three months away and worries about his family

cramped in a small cabin with only so much food. But then he forces himself
to think beyond winter to spring, when they will boil maple sap into sugar
as the winter wheat and forest leeks sprout. He pictures more and more of the
big trees crashing down, the heads of the trapped and shot cougar and
wolves turned in for bounty, the sunlight and crops and livestock. And in
this story he is telling himself in the summer of 1825, he is certain that soon
he will have enough profit to build a proper frame house near the north line
of the lot, where the land company says it will someday be cutting a road.
His own farm and frame house. His own man. As he grips his musket and
stands up unsteadily to urinate on the roaring fire, he can see that his good
friend is still awake and says, David, even though the ground ain't the best,
I think we done picked pretty good when all we had to go by was a map and
a compass and a dream. Don't you?

American Dreams

To the boys of Pendleton, our blue-collar fathers and uncles and grandfathers were Audie Murphy the war hero and John L. Lewis the labor hero rolled into one. If not for the men who had put down their tools and joined the army, we boys would have saluted the swastika crisply each morning in school instead of muttering to the Stars and Stripes; or would have been speaking grammatical Japanese instead of ungrammatical English. If not for the unions and the strikes before and after the war, we would have been living in industrial slums instead of in a bedroom community where the streets were safe and freezers full; if not for the factories and mills where the workers kept the owners and bosses in line, there would be no presents for Christmas. We knew a dramatic blue-collar outline of history, and believed that because of our brave and hardworking fathers and uncles and grandfathers, the dreams of every American could come true.

The steel mills of western New York could no longer compete with the mills of the defeated Japanese, and factories of all sorts were moving south where the crackers were willing to work for peanuts. But to us boys, to us American sons of the Rust Belt, the image of smoke billowing from a factory stack still rivaled the flag as a proud national symbol. Our male elders made the smoke, and yet within the parenthesis of our boyhood faith, in Pendleton, the air was still clean.

If we had lived in Pendleton twenty years earlier, we might have labored alongside the men in the barns and fields of old homesteads. But most of the barns were now empty and sagging, and most of the fields abandoned to weeds and brush; in a stream of traffic, our fathers traveled to and from factories that few of us ever saw. Unlike the real Audie Murphy and John L. Lewis, our fathers were anonymous heroes. But we boys knew that with their own hands our fathers manufactured the cars and buses and gasoline; built the roads and bridges; generated the electricity that lit our school; made the chairs we sat upon bored all day. They had the hands of heroes. The palms and fingers of our male elders were stained and scarred and callused from winning the war and making the buses and cars and gasoline and bridges and electricity and chairs of America.

And sometimes it seemed that so, too, were their souls.

We loved them and knew that they loved us. But we also feared them. What right-minded boy would not fear the disapproval of Audie Murphy and John L. Lewis? Who among us was worthy of their grace? Our fathers were usually away earning a paycheck, busy with household repairs, or transported somewhere by beer and television. But if one of the men was working outside, his sweaty back rippling as he repaired the lawn mower or hoed the vegetable garden, we tried to behave or took our mischief into someone else's yard. I once saw a burly teenager get knocked cold in midsentence as he talked back to his smaller father. We boys saw the men work around the house and watch television and drink and glare and throw knockout punches in our bedroom community, but we did not see them laboring in smoggy Lackawanna and Lockport and Niagara Falls and Buffalo and Depew and Tonawanda as they earned our sustenance in the sweltering and filthy flour and steel mills and automobile and chemical plants a world away from the clean houses and shaded yards of their homes, their castles.

It was enough that these heroes were our fathers.

It was during a thunderstorm and our fathers were somewhere else. Several of us boys were in the hay loft of the old wooden barn on the edge of abandoned farmland behind the Schroeder house. Charlie Schroeder was describing the death of a barn kitten. Several days earlier, from atop an old pile of bales that almost reached the rough-hewn beams of the roof, the kitten had leapt reflexively at a sparrow flying past, falling to the wooden floor. Now Charlie dared any of us to retrieve a pigeon egg from the nest far out on a beam that ran high along the wall.

At age ten I was neither brave nor foolish enough to accept his dare. Nor were any of the others. So Charlie had to take it himself.

He stepped out onto the thick beam from atop bales piled against a wall of the loft. Chest touching the dark splintery wall boards, he slowly slid to his left, feet shuffling sideways a few inches at a time.

As he neared the nest, a pigeon swooped at him. One of us yelled, "Look out!"

Charlie froze for a second. Then he continued his sideways shuffle.

Inch by inch, he slid farther out onto the beam, and second by second the distance to the floor seemed to grow. Then he was an arm's length away. He began to hunch down, thighs spreading and knees bending, right hand pressing against a rough wide board above his head, left hand reaching down toward the nest, outstretched fingers still inches from the egg.

But then he made the mistake of looking down at the floor. And he saw the dark stain where the kitten had died bleeding from its mouth and ears. Abruptly, he straightened up—and lost and recovered his balance as his rapt audience cried out in unison.

As we held our breath, he tried to flatten his rigid torso against the wall. He turned his face away from the nest and pressed his cheek against the wood, mouth puckered, nose askew, eyes bulging and unblinking. He ceased moving. Several seconds passed, and still he was frozen.

Someone managed to ask, "Are you okay?"

Charlie didn't reply. Boys began to shout—forget the egg, just come back, you can do it, are you okay, say something. But he would neither speak nor move. I couldn't bare to speak. I was thinking about the James Phillips Who Fell.

Bob and Mark Schroeder climbed down from the loft and ran to the house for help.

The pigeon was swooping so close that Charlie must have felt the breeze of its wings on the exposed side of his face.

When Mr. Schroeder entered, all of us still in the loft began to yell to him at once. He ordered us to stay quiet and we instantly obeyed. Now he was Audie Murphy and John L. Lewis and my father and Paul Keller's and Andy Strout's as he slid fearlessly along the beam while quietly warning Charlie not to look down and over and over assuring him that now he was safe. We knew he was. We knew we were. Our fathers extended their left hands and the sons took hold with their rights. And the unworthy led by the worthy, all of us began the slow sideways trip back to safety.

In my neighborhood, I had two groups of playmates. The Strout, Keller, and Schroeder boys fought a lot with their fists and played war with horse chestnuts, rocks, and BBs. My second, gentler set of playmates included David Nasca, who was the top student in his grade, and Johnny Burbidge, whose mother made him take piano lessons. When I played with David and Johnny instead of the other group, the battles normally were waged with toy rifles. We stalked or waited in ambush until someone shouted, "Blam! Blam! You're dead!" The slaughtered boy's weapon was flung loose as he fell screaming onto his back, twisting and kicking and then silent and still, arms and legs spread wide.

Now the vanquisher's gunfire had given away his hiding spot in an apple tree. He jumped down and sprinted across the yard, around the house, down the short hill. And just as he flopped onto his belly to crawl safely into the field of goldenrod, he heard "Blam! Blam! Blam! You're dead!" And with a gaping wound, the doomed writhed in dying agony, careful not to roll on dog shit. He imagined his mother's grief when the telegram arrived.

After we had played war one fall afternoon, in his kitchen David told Johnny and me how his father had received his wound in World War II. I told how my Uncle Al had received his. Then David brought out his father's purple heart and the small black-and-white photographs taken after Mr. Nasca's platoon had helped liberate a death camp: the mountains of Jewish dead, naked hairless skin draped over bones, the blankly open eyes fixed on us. Stoked by rage, we gulped down the rest of our hot chocolate, pulled on our jackets, and ran outside to kill each other all over again in the great war that the generation of our fathers had won against evil, each of us a GI and the others Krauts. In the middle of our battle, which no longer seemed real enough, we cast down our plastic guns and hurled apples at each other's heads.

When the weather turned arctic we left the Nazis to the Russians. Occasionally we sledded down the icy runs we had sprayed with hoses, but on most days the cold kept us inside where we argued with our sisters, were forced by our mothers to clean our rooms, and watched television hour after hour. Even the Schroeders, Strouts, and Kellers had taken their quarrels inside.

Each weekday afternoon at 3:30, I jumped down from the yellow school bus and ran across my snowy yard. In the kitchen I threw down my coat and books and gulped a snack and then stretched out on the living room carpet to watch reruns of *Superman* and *Highway Patrol.* After supper, the family—except Dad when he was working overtime—settled near the television, speechless and still except to hurry to the bathroom or refrigerator during commercials peddling floor wax, pickup trucks, antacid, orange juice, beer, potato chips, soup, cigarettes, insurance, together in our separateness in the life-and-death glare and blare of chase, guns, disaster narrowly escaped: *Wagon Train, Combat, The Virginian, Gunsmoke.* For humor we had *The Beverly Hillbillies* and for wholesomeness *The Lawrence Welk Show.*

Sometimes when I woke late at night and was shuffling to the bathroom, I would hear the television whining and find Dad asleep with a test pattern casting a sickly gray light over his face. There would be an open jar of salve for his welding burns lined up with several empty beer bottles on the carpet next to the easy chair. I would call out and shake him and bang together brown bottles, gradually rousing him from numbing dreams.

I was ten the spring that the power company assigned my father to three weeks of long shifts at a different plant. My mother had to shake him awake at six instead of seven so that he would have time for the sixty-mile drive to the factory town of Dunkirk. Wearing only white cotton underpants, he shuffled into the kitchen stubbly-faced and puffy-eyed and clumsily extracted a cigarette from the pack of L&Ms on the table, then sat down and lit up as steam rose from the tea before him. In her heavy cotton nightgown, Mom buttered and sliced his toast on the counter, and then walked it over on a small plastic plate and stooped to kiss him on the cheek. First he smoked the cigarette and then sipped tea and finally ate the cold toast. Then he shuffled into the bathroom to unburden himself of last night's beer.

As she lifted away the plate and teacup, Mom could hear the splashing of his urine streaming into the toilet water, and then the faucet running, his short hair still dark and face still boyish in the small mirror above the sink filling with hot water as he lathered up. She heard the slurping draining sound when he finished shaving and heard the faucet go on again as he rinsed away the ring of lather and whiskers from the sink. She finished packing his lunch box, a fresh tomato and stalk of celery and two liverwurst sandwiches and a piece of chocolate cake and a salt shaker and fork and Thermos of tea and two napkins, and heard him brushing his teeth and rinsing, and then he came out still in his underpants but lifting his feet now and went into the bedroom where she had set out his clothing folded neatly next to their wedding picture on the painted dresser.

She kissed him good-bye and he went out with his gray plastic lunch box after he heard the honking in the driveway of our mortgaged house in Pendleton. The man on the passenger side of the front seat was already asleep, slid down with his head leaned against the cool window, and the driver nodded. "Morning, Jim."

"Hey, Roy."

In back Dad smoked another L&M and listened to Clint Buehlman on the radio chatter about the traffic and weather with his soothing voice between songs by Bing Crosby and Bobby Darin. With his feet still on the floor, Dad stretched out a little on the seat to sleep while Roy drove and smoked Pall Malls and sipped black coffee from a Thermos cup.

In the country outside of Dunkirk, rows of grapevines sloped gently to the shore of Lake Erie, whose whitecaps were visible all the way out to the gray horizon. Then the vineyards gave way to industrial development, and Roy turned up the radio volume and momentarily hit the brakes and said, "Almost time for work, boys! Get your lazy asses up!"

My father liked working at the Dunkirk plant. The company had selected him for his skill to work in a crew that was over-hauling boilers. He received extra pay, but best of all he got to pull on his dark gray welding hood in front of the Dunkirk men who needed his help. Even with the hood still flipped up he was set apart from the others with their bright yellow hard hats and exposed faces. When he was ready, he flipped it down, his face hidden by the dark glass. And as the others went about their routine tasks they had to avert their eyes from the blinding arc, as if in shame, while the beckoned stranger plied his skill in mystery.

After a ten-hour shift and shower and dinner out and the long ride, he wasn't home again until we kids were asleep for the night. He went in to look at April in her crib before he sat down in his easy chair with a bottle of beer.

In the American dream, every child grows up to have a more comfortable life than did his parents, although in the nightmare that was my fifth-grade education, my grades left no room for comfort. My father and his buddies at the plant made fun of the college-educated supervisors and engineers, the "pretty boys in white shirts" who were "afraid to get their hands dirty," who were "born with silver spoons," and who had so little common sense that "they need to read a book before they can tie their shoes." But like most other coal- or grease-soiled laborers, Dad expected his children to earn college degrees. The American dream demanded it.

My grades suggested I was not the sharpest tool in the shed, not college material. And my teacher's comments on my recent report card confirmed Dad's suspicion that I was an under-achiever: "Mark has taken to not finishing his work, often wanders around the room and talks a great deal. He seldom has his place in reading or whatever we are doing. I have warned him about this but so far no improvement has been shown."

Even at home, I neglected my work. When washing the supper dishes, I spent more time playing in the water than scrubbing pots; when Dad was home, his glare could boil the soapy water as I loafed. I threw my dirty clothing on my bedroom floor instead of in the hamper. And soon after the snow melted in April, Dad made the mistake of ordering me to shovel our German shepherd's exposed and thawed crap off the lawn: I managed to smear more of it over the grass than I got onto the shovel and into the trash bag. Then the bag ripped and leaked while I was dragging it around the lawn instead of lifting and carrying it, so I had to start over again. By the time I stopped working, our front yard looked as if it had been the wintering place for a herd of dysenteric buffalo. The disaster earned me a weekend of angry paternal silence.

I had what the delicate call "a poor work ethic," but in my working-class family and community, laziness was considered to be the ax murderer of hope. It didn't matter if his job was filthy and deafening and sweaty and stupefying and dangerous and insecure and low-paying; the blue-collar worker remained convinced that hard work was a virtue. Although it might not improve his own life, his hard work would benefit his kids. They would attend college.

In my family, to say that a child was lazy was to worry that he might end up on welfare, the supreme shame. Dad's family had received public assistance while his father's broken ribs had healed from an injury incurred on a construction job, a time when the family had run so low on heating fuel that Dad and his brothers had needed to walk railroad tracks to gather whatever spilled coal they could find. But in Dad's opinion, public assistance had become downright alluring since then, a siren to the lazy. It was imperative to save his son from the shame of welfare before it was too late. Unfortunately, he worked too much overtime and was too weary to properly supervise me as I did chores around the house. And by his reckoning I was too much at risk, too close to becoming a terminally lazy welfare recipient, to be entrusted solely to my mother or any other woman.

Fortunately, Mom's barrel-chested, callus-handed father was in need of a helper during my Easter vacation. Grandfather Wagner was a full-time road worker for the state, ran his farm without help except in haying season, and each year cut and split and sold more than a hundred cord of firewood. Although earlier that spring he had broken an ankle while jumping from a road grader after its brakes had failed on a hill, by Easter he felt healed enough to begin hobbling around the swampy woods where he had purchased the right to cut the firewood. Because it was important that he not tear or puncture the several layers of plastic sheeting and utility tape protecting his cast, he needed someone to fetch the gas can and tools and to pile chunks of wood and to drag away branches that were too thin to become firewood.

To my father's surprise, I was excited that I would be spending several days of my vacation at work with my grandfather. In my family, Grandfather's reputation for hard work was so strong that I felt as if I had been selected to aid Paul Bunyan in his time of distress. I was certain that by earning a dollar per hour, I was about to become the richest ten year old in Pendleton. And I would be working in the woods, where I would be safe from my father, who had been working a lot of overtime.

About thirty miles east of Buffalo, the doomed woods bordered muddy Tonawanda Creek as it meandered through the flat soggy country beyond the Tonawanda Indian Reservation. As Grandfather navigated the tractor up the rutty lane, the loose tire chains rattled and slung up clumps of partially frozen mud, and tools thumped and rolled around in the wooden trailer. I stood unsteadily behind the metal seat, desperately clutching the woolen jacket stretched tight across his broad back. It was difficult for him to operate the clutch with his left ankle and foot in a cast, and his laughter roared over the barking and popping of the engine when a lurching change of gears caused me to hold on tighter as we bounced deeper into the gray woods. He was in a hurry. "By God," he yelled back to me, "the sun's coming up and we ain't even started work yet! Lost time! Lost time! We'll just have to work harder to make up for lost time, Markie."

I had barely climbed down after him when his chain saw barked and screamed. Chewing into a tree, the snarling saw spewed wood chips and sawdust and belched oily smoke that slowly drifted away through the cold still woods. Soon I could see the top branches of the tree begin to sway slightly. Then with a prolonged whining and cracking that rose above the snarl of the saw engine, the tree began to fall slowly and then with a plummeting blur as Grandfather continued to guide the saw bar. Dead branches exploded into pieces, and the thick bole hit the ground with a bouncing crash that I could feel through the bottom of my boots a hundred feet away.

He called me closer as he prepared to fell the next tree. I could see his breath in the cold air as he explained how to study the branches and bole to determine which direction the tree "wants to fall." Then he demonstrated how to cut a hinge to prevent the tree from slipping off the stump toward the wood-cutter like an enormous battering ram as it fell. Before dropping the tree, he warned me to always thump a bole with the head of an ax and to listen carefully to the sound before beginning to cut: hollow trees were widow makers that might fall in any di-rection. But he added that because he liked honey so much, he himself never let a hollow tree stand; he once took a hundred pounds of honey from a single cavity. And after a hollow tree did fall in an unexpected direction and "hung up" on a nearby tree, he showed me how to "walk it down" by cutting off lengths of the bole from the underside while keeping the saw bar perpendicular to the ground.

He turned to lopping off the smaller branches of the felled trees, which he directed me to heap so that he could "come back next winter with my gun and chase some rabbit stew out of them brush piles." Next he began cutting the larger branches and the boles into eighteen-inch chunks. He showed me how to pile wood, but the best I could do with the larger chunks was to roll them to the edge of a pile where eventually Grandfather would do the lifting. After he had finished sharpening the teeth of the saw chain with a round file, he watched me for a while, laughed at my struggles, and said, "What'sa matter? When I was your age, I could carry two of those at the same time. Got a bad back or something?"

"I just can't lift the big ones."

"You won't get no muscles sitting in front of the TV, Markie. You sure won't get none that way."

"I help shovel the driveway."

At that he simply laughed and yanked the cord to restart the saw.

Eventually we took off our coats and hats and had to slosh around in mud and water as the sun rose higher in the blue sky over the thawing woods, which was just beginning to leaf out. And although by noon his woolen shirt was soaked with sweat, Grandfather built a small fire so that we could toast our sandwiches on forked sticks and warm the slab of bacon left over from breakfast.

As he finished gulping down his lunch, he crumpled the wax paper and tossed it into the fire. Then he began to talk, as he often did, about his childhood in Michigan. Gazing into the woods as he summoned memories and words, he described his fright when he had first heard the nocturnal yowl of a bobcat.

I asked if his father had ever shot one, what Grandpa called a wildcat. "I don't think none of us ever even saw one. All you did was see their tracks and hear them. You never saw one. They were like ghosts."

I asked if wildcats lived in the woods we were cutting. "Not no more," he said. He added that "way back," many of the trees had been too large for a man to reach halfway around the trunk, and the forest had been home to bobcats, cougars, wolves, rattlesnakes, bears, Indians. Then the Indians had been conquered, the trees clearcut, the land farmed. "You can tell. Ground's almost even: smoothed out by plowing. No humps and hollows where trees blew down. Farmed land, for sure." Then the acreage had been abandoned, perhaps because the site was too wet. The woods had grown back for us to cut.

"Where did the animals go when the big woods got cut down?"

He snorted and replied, "Money! They turned into money. Furs and bounties. Meat sold to city people. Money. Just like these trees right here."

A few seconds later, he yawned, stretched his thick arms above his bald head, and said, "It's too bad you gotta grow up where there's not even a woods big enough to get lost in. Is your Dad still thinking about buying a cabin in the hills?"

"I guess so." I shrugged. "I dunno. I'm not sure."

"Must be he's thinking it would be good to get you lost." When Grandfather was done slapping his thighs and laughing at his joke, he stood up from the log and pulled a watch from the deep front pocket of his denim overalls. "Twelve-thirty! You better hurry up and get back to work. I'll have to dock you a dollar, Markie!"

Back at the farmhouse that evening, I ate heartily and then took a long bath in the cast-iron tub. I dried off quickly and stood damp and naked before the mirror to check my sore body for new muscles.

I was too tired to watch television and by seven o'clock had climbed atop the thick saggy mattress of the squeaky guest bed where I almost immediately fell asleep to the ticking of the big windup alarm clock set for five in the morning.

Now and then when the baby was asleep, my tired father would urge my tired mother, "Forget that cleaning. Sit down and relax." Mom then fidgeted while reading the newspaper or watching television, but would shortly resume scrubbing and polishing, and he wouldn't mention it again until another evening. He had also stopped badgering me to do better in

school, and no longer asked to see my homework and corrected
tests. With another child to clothe and feed, he was working all
the overtime he could get. Now at home all he seemed to care
about were TV and beer and sleep.

He was too tired to scold me about my shortcomings un-
prompted, but his weary withdrawal worried me. His vitality
had flowed into the power lines, brightening or heating other
people's homes.

When it came to attention from our parents, Kim and I felt as
if we were fighting over scarce food. We began to bicker over
everything from which television shows we would watch to
which of us would sit in which chair at the kitchen table. She
made fun of my plummeting grades and I of her soaring weight.
Increasingly, we settled our quarrels with fists and feet and
teeth and fingernails. We disturbed our exhausted father like
kamikazes. He gave up trying to determine which of us was
at fault and began to punish us both. "You better move your
hands away from your ass," he would bark when he was
about to strap one of us, but I couldn't, and my hands and
arms absorbed the blows. The strapping became so frequent
that he drove a nail into the kitchen wall and hung from it a
warning belt.

As if she were the infant, Kim began pissing her pants. And
late one evening when April was crying in Mom's arms, Kim shit
herself. Mom handed the baby to me and screamed at Kim until
Dad got up from his easy chair and said, "I'll call the goddamn
adoption agency right now and tell them to come get her."

Mom swept Kim up in her arms and wept. His objective ac-
complished, Dad returned to the living room.

In his easy chair, he leaned back into the dreaming position.

During the second afternoon, Horace Guild gets to thinking about winter again. He is sharpening his ax and thinking about his wife and children cramped in a cabin in the wilderness as the wind blows and snow falls. As he worries about his family, sweat drips off the end of his nose and falls onto the bleeding stump where he is filing the ax. All around him, steam rises from the forest floor where the moist humus is now exposed to direct sunlight.

He straightens up with a groan, his palms pressing against the hollow of his back, and begins counting again. He counts stumps. Next he subtracts the number of trees he has cut. And yes, he is still working harder than David. In two days, he has felled four more trees. And there is David on his hands and knees again, drinking from the spring again like a deer, not working again. And with his belly too full of water again, David stands up and wipes his lips with his sleeve and stands there. Resting again.

Burping again.

"Hibner, if you ain't gonna do your share, maybe I'll just start back for home."

David spins, and they look into each other's glare.

Then without warning, David smiles. And at that, they begin to laugh harder than at any time since striking out into the wilderness.

Wild Urges

Life in my home was beginning to feel like those afternoons in my neighborhood when we boys threw down our toys guns and pelted each other with apples or stones, but without the laughter. Kim and I went on bickering and fighting, and our parents became increasingly impatient and exhausted. Dad was still working all the overtime he could get. He often fell asleep in his easy chair while Mom was warming his supper, and was quick to reach for the belt when awakened. He glared with moist reddened eyes, and I imagined steamy smoke rising from his ears. And yet I didn't blame our familial combat on my father's necessary job or on the new baby I loved to hold and make grin. Instead, with the encouragement of my Sunday school teacher, I began to suspect that a small demon had moved into my home, and into me in particular.

Maybe it wasn't my family's fault.

Maybe I was possessed by an imp.

One afternoon this imp prodded the left side of my face from the inside, causing my lips to purse and curl askew toward my squinting left eye. Within days the imp was making mischief throughout my being. Without yet knowing why, I rapidly blinked and shrugged. I took rapid, shallow breaths until I hyperventilated. I grunted. I furiously tapped the floor with my heels. I threw back my head and squeaked while my fists smacked my bruised abdomen. I struggled with urges to leap out a second-story window or run in front of a moving car or stick my fingers into the churning blades of an electric cake mixer. And sometimes I became speechless in the middle of a conversation as I suddenly and vividly imagined that the person I had been talking with was bleeding from his nose and ears.

One morning a girl sitting across from me on the school bus asked, "Why do you do that with your eyes and shoulders and make those noises?" But I couldn't answer her: she was bleeding from her nose and ears. Anyhow, I didn't know why, nor did the doctor to whom my mother had taken me: "He's a nervous child," he had mistakenly concluded. "They're just bad habits."

I became so accustomed to the imp's antics that often I was unaware of the tics until someone called my attention to them. Children mocked me, and Dad sometimes informed me of a tic by slapping my head. On one occasion, when my shocked father was witnessing a tic he hadn't seen before—my tongue slowly slipping out of my mouth, snaking over my upper lip, stretching toward the end of my nose as my head slowly tipped back—he yelled, "Eva, come into the living room!" As she hurried in from the kitchen, he said, "You gotta see his new habit."

But I denied the display. Once I became aware of a tic I could suppress it, the urges welling up in waves until I found a private place where I would blink and shrug and contort my face and tap the floor and tip back my head and punch my stomach and squeak and hyperventilate and let my tongue slither until I regained temporary control over my body.

I had Tourette syndrome: a neurobiological condition caused by a genetically inherited imbalance in one or more of the chemicals that serve as transmitters between neurons in the brain. But when I was a boy I didn't know any of that, and it was my Sunday school teacher who, by reaching back into the Middle Ages, gave my condition a diagnosis that I somewhat welcomed.

One morning as I waited in the church vestibule for Sunday school to begin, the imp compelled me to pull on the thick rope that rose into the high darkness of the old steeple and I yanked hard and fast until the rope repeatedly lifted me off my feet and set me down as the heavy bell swung, the surrounding neighborhood barraged by clanging. Eventually the urge to ring the bell was exhausted, but I was the last child to walk down the steep narrow stairs to the church cellar where classes were held behind portable partitions.

The students were seated on metal folding chairs arranged in short rows on the bare concrete floor. As I sat down, my teacher interrupted her lecture about the Sermon on the Mount to ask, "Class, what do you think would have happened if someone had rung a bell so loudly that Jesus couldn't be heard that day on the mount? Would we know His word today? Would we be saved? I'd ask Mark the question, but he's late again and probably hasn't read our assignment again, and so he wouldn't have the slightest idea what our topic is. Would he now?"

Having shamed me, and without waiting for anyone to respond to her absurd questions, she resumed teaching: she explained that to gain the wisdom He preached on the mount, Jesus had spent forty days in the wilderness where—she said while staring at me—He had withstood the devil's temptations. She added that He, following His stay in the wilderness and while the multitude followed Him across Galilee, cured lunatics and people with palsy and cast demons out of the possessed.

My Sunday school book was a collection of illustrated and condensed Biblical stories that interested me even less than my teacher's lectures, but now, with her eyes fixed on me as she described how Jesus had cast out demons, I became interested in her lecture and wished I had read the assignment. Her implication made sense. And despite my hatred of whatever made me tic, I was rather relieved to hear that it might be a demon, an imp. Didn't that mean my tics were caused by a sort of supernatural tapeworm, and not by my own weakness?

For several months, mocked by other children and occasionally my own father, I felt like an outcast. I was ashamed and lonely and full of self-pity. I believed I was already living in hell, so what more harm could come from making an acquaintance there?

I decided to skip the church service that followed Sunday school. I walked home with Bob Schroeder. He offered to share his cigarette with me, and I accepted, urged by the demon, the imp, who was tantalized by the addictive substitution of smoke for air, the breezy exhaling, the repetitive flicking of ash. But then I thought, What if someone sees me smoking and tells Dad? A week earlier, I took a drag on a smoldering butt he had just tossed away; failing to get the joke, he forced me to eat it. Now, recalling my retching, I returned the cigarette to Bob without having put it to my mouth. "Suit yourself," he said. He took a deep drag. And agitating the imp for the rest of the day, he blew smoke at me.

When I arrived home from church, I was relieved to find that Dad was still catching up on his sleep. I gulped down a glass of pop and a scoop of ice cream. Still wearing my Sunday clothing and shoes and clutching a slingshot and a brown grocery bag bulging with glass jars, I hiked into the field behind my house.

Emerging from a row of brush, I flushed a pair of mallards and a flock of redwing blackbirds out of the cattails of a farm pond just ahead. The quacking ducks circled twice before I lost sight of them in the sun's glare, and in the distance the redwings swirled around a dead tree, then alighted a few at a time on the bare branches, their screeching softening. Squatting on the muddy bank, I removed a jar from the grocery bag and threw it into the pond. I slung several stones with the slingshot before one hit and shattered the glass. Within an hour all of the jars had become shards on the bottom of the muddy pond.

I sat down on the bank, shrugging and grunting. As the frogs gradually resumed croaking, the imp compelled me to capture one. I dropped the slingshot and waded into the water and muck, pushing through thick cattails, ruining my shoes and soaking the pants Mom had painstakingly ironed that morning. With frightened croaks, frog after frog leapt away and zigzagged along the soft bottom, leaving a cloudy trail. I lunged at a bullfrog, stumbled, and fell face first into the water. I stood up cursing, wiping my eyes, and resumed the hunt.

Eventually I spotted a leopard frog with its hind legs submerged and the rest of its body exposed on the shore. It had the lusterless appearance of death, but something, which I took to be breathing, was causing movement under its skin—and I seized the frog with both hands. And the decaying flesh exploded, flinging maggots into my face.

Our house was on Bear Ridge, which rose narrowly and incongruously above the dominant flatness of Pendleton. From our yard, I could look across the road and see a half-mile stretch of abandoned farmland, then a small woods—to me a distant and unexplored wilderness. Desiring a new life, I decided to explore this wilderness, maybe stake a claim. And certain that the original bears of Bear Ridge must still survive in such a place, I took along my Daisy BB gun for protection.

On still nights I could hear the deep metallic rumbling of trains, so I knew that railroad tracks ran through the woods. But I was surprised to find that the town's main drainage ditch ran alongside the tracks. I felt as if I had discovered the Mississippi or Amazon. With a canteen of Kool-Aid swinging from my belt and with my pockets stuffed with melting chocolate chips filched from Mom's pantry, I picked my way along the brushy bank of the wide ditch, my eyes peeled for bears and BB gun cocked. For much of the summer, I explored the wilderness of Pendleton while my father labored long hours in the power plant, longing for the Alleghenies.

Gradually I grew disappointed not to have encountered any bears or even a deer. One day, as I spotted Kim in our backyard bending over to pick a flower, I let my imagination and anger get the better of me. I shot her in the ass. She ran howling into the house. I lied to Dad, tearfully claiming that the shooting had been an accident. He believed me, so I wasn't strapped. But he did judge me careless and took away my weapon for the rest of the summer.

When Mom pointed out to him that I seldom had playmates, Dad became alarmed. "You need to spend more time around other boys," he said, and ordered me to join the Little League even though the baseball season had already started. He'd never once played catch with me. Instead of pointing this out to him, I told him that I didn't like baseball and never participated in the neighborhood games. "You'll learn," he replied.

When it was my turn to bat during my first practice, I planted my feet directly on home plate. The coach was able to teach me the correct batting stance, but he couldn't help me in the outfield. I circled beneath a high fly ball, my cap slipping off before the baseball thudded onto my forehead. For a few dizzy moments I didn't mind playing baseball, but after practice I told Dad that I wanted to quit the team. He wouldn't permit it.

When my second-place team was four runs ahead in the final inning of a game against the first-place team, my coach sent me into the lineup. In right field, I lost the game by muffing two hopping ground balls, one of which careened off my crotch. After the game, my furious teammates hurled insults at me while Dad and I hurried to the car parked on the yellow grass.

As he braked in our driveway, Dad asked if I still wanted to quit the team. My face was contorting and shoulders shrugging, the stressed imp higher on chemicals than usual. Dad looked very tired and sad and I wanted to tell him that I would stay on the team and become the next Mickey Mantle. But my balls were still aching, and I answered, "Yes." Without saying anything further, he climbed out of the car and walked into the house.

I remained in the car for a few more minutes. Then, rather than walk through the front doorway and chance hearing my father announce to my mother that I was a quitter and failure, I entered the house through the cellar doorway. Near the oil furnace, above a wooden stool and chained to a metal frame bolted to the ceiling, hung a punching bag that Dad had bought for me several weeks earlier. I had yet to slug it. But now I stepped onto the stool, and flailed the leather bag until my arms hung leaden at my sides.

After noticing how much time I was spending with the punching bag, Dad decided that I could use a body bag as well. On a Saturday when he wasn't working overtime, he filled a burlap sack with rags and sand while kneeling on the bare concrete floor of our basement, and told me a story about the James Phillips in Ireland who was his grandfather's brother, who "learned to fight before he learned to run." Whenever the boy's father went into the nearby village of Drumbo, he took along this James. After locating some tough-looking lad of about the same age, he'd ask, "Think ye can beat that one?"

James, who was small for his age, would stride up to the other boy and knock him down. When James was ten, one of his older brothers, who was sick of being thrashed by a runty sibling, had clobbered him with a hammer. Eventually James came out of the coma, but his skull was permanently dented. When he returned to school, it was discovered that he could no longer read or write.

His father stopped encouraging him to fight, but James fought more than ever. By the time he was sixteen he was fighting for pay in country pubs. Each Friday evening a circling crowd of men pressed the combatants, hollering and cheering, betting, clutching mugs of foamy black beer, some of them kicking out through the smoke at the boxers who fought bareknuckled without break until one of the combatants—seldom James—had been knocked senseless to the dirt floor. It was said that James could feel no pain. He became known as the Ulster Bantam Rooster, graduated to the pubs of Belfast, and even made a brief tour of seedy London pubs.

In his twenties, he gave up boxing and sailed for North America in search of a better life that he never did find. He stayed three years in Canada and the United States, returning to Ireland before the James Phillipses in America began to die young. He took any backbreaking job he could find in the countryside around Drumbo, building stone walls or scything wheat or plowing stony fields from dawn to dusk, attacking work with the same dogged insensate ferocity with which he had boxed. And he labored, illiterate and broken-headed, until he died in his eighties.

"I thought he died when he fell?"

"A different James. This man was the uncle of the James who fell."

"It's hard to keep all of them straight."

"Same endings, I guess. Same endings."

I felt guilty about fantasizing that the body bag was Dad, so usually I pretended that it was some boy or another who had mocked me, his ugly face I bloodied, his soft stomach I punished in fury, until one evening when the burlap sprung a leak and gushed sand. Mom cleaned up the mess, but the bag was never repaired.

One afternoon when Kim and I were riding home on the yellow bus, I found an excuse to ply my new skill.

The bus engine growled and gears ground, brakes screeched, doors swished open and closed, and escapees sprinted across lawns with the odor of diesel fuel clinging to their clothing. The yet imprisoned popped up their middle fingers as they leaned out the windows of the bouncing screaming cursing laughing shouting kissing punching spit-wad-throwing canned jungle of yahoos.

I was sharing a seat with a new boy in the neighborhood. Because of his physical resemblance to the comic strip character, he had been nicknamed Dondie. We were becoming friends, but now, turned around in the seat in front of us, Kim was testing the limits of my friendship. What began as teasing between her and Dondie was now a contest of meanness. His voice stretched high as he called her fat. After a hurt laugh she called him bony and ugly and added that it was no wonder his mother had to live with his grandparents—that his father was away because he was ashamed of having a son who is in a comic strip.

Dondie lived across the street from us, so he climbed off the bus when we did. He planted his feet on the edge of the road and stung Kim's plump shoulder with his bony right fist. She dropped wailing to the gravel.

Before I knew it I was sitting on his chest, pummeling his face. When his cry was louder than Kim's, I freed him and he ran into his grandparents' house. Kim tearfully thanked me. I didn't reply, didn't help her up. I just stood there, surprised at myself.

Surprised, but suddenly confident in my capacity for violence.

A few days after I thrashed Dondie, my sixth-grade teacher was in the hallway talking with another teacher when the class bully left his seat and punched me on the back of my head. Before he could return to his seat, I tackled him; girls screamed and the teacher strode back into the room, lifted us to our feet, and banged our heads together.

And it was as if, in the clunking of heads, I had exchanged brains with the bully. Over the weekend, I waylaid Johnny Burbidge as he walked past my home on his way to play with someone else, and beat him up simply because I desired to witness him run howling home.

About a week after bruising my forehead, my teacher was beckoned into the hallway by another teacher. When he returned to the classroom, he was weeping. He told the class that the president had been shot.

On television during the hours and days ahead, I repeatedly saw Jackie in her blood-stained dress, Ruby shoot Oswald, the long gray funeral march behind the horse-drawn hearse, John John and little Caroline at the grave. And Dad kept muttering, "What is this country coming to?"

During Christmas vacation, I played in the deep snow drifts behind our house where Bear Ridge sloped to the lake plain. With my gloved hands and a round-nose shovel, I dug a tunnel and chambers. After sunset I lit my hideaway with candles. Across the road, on the opposite slope of Bear Ridge, neighborhood children tobogganed and threw snowballs. But from my snow cave I couldn't hear their laughter and shouts, and was glad—as glad as I was that Dad was away working overtime. I read Hardy Boys mysteries by candlelight and ate graham crackers and pretended that I was tunneling out of a Jap prison camp.

One night as I came into the house, blind Grandma Phillips, whose children were still caring for her in turns, asked me if it was cold outside. I replied, "Not in my cave." She asked to touch my face. I stood in front of her rocking chair. Slowly and lightly she moved her fingers over my chin, lips, runny nose, glowing cheeks—and then, closing and stilling them, over my furiously blinking eyes.

I turned around to see that Dad was finally home from work, still clutching his lunch pail, studying his blind son and insightful mother.

Grandma Phillips died in her sleep when I was eleven. For a month after the funeral, Dad refused overtime, and on a Friday evening asked me if I wanted to spend the weekend fishing and camping on Ischua Creek. I shrugged. I didn't even look away from the television. From the couch Mom said, "Mark, didn't you hear Daddy? You're gonna get to go fishing and camping with him."

"He doesn't act too crazy about it."

"Oh, he wants to go. Don't you, Mark?"

From my spot on the rug I looked over at Mom sitting on the couch, but not at Dad pushed back in his easy chair. I feared his anger and glares and belt, and wondered what we would have to talk about other than my tics, poor grades, misbehavior, and general laziness. Yet I could see the urgency on Mom's face, and I replied, "I guess so. I'll go if you want."

"You see? He wants to go." She was grinning and nodding excessively. "It'll be fun. You guys won't wanna come back."

Next to me on the rug, Kim asked, "Can I go, too?"

"Oh no, I'd miss you too much. April and I would be too lonely here all alone," Mom said.

"You and April can come, too."

"We'll bake a big chocolate cake while they're away. We'll eat the whole thing ourselves."

"You gotta save me a piece," I said.

"Mommy said no."

"That's not fair!"

"Is fair! Is fair!"

"Is not!"

"Knock it off! Turn up the TV. I can't hear a thing. Mark—go get me another beer."

I was in bed when I heard the stairs creaking and then Mom knocking on my door and asking to come in. My bed dipped as she sat down on the edge, the white ceiling and her face flashing bright as out on Bear Ridge Road a car whizzed by our house. She asked, "Do you feel all right?"

"Yes."

"You wanna go with Daddy, don't you?"

"I dunno."

"What's wrong?"

"I dunno."

"That last time when you guys went fishing you couldn't sleep the night before, you were so excited. How come you're not excited this time?"

I tried to recall why I had been excited about the Niagara River trip that had followed Grandpa's death, but it was like thinking about a different father and different son. Under the covers, I shrugged. "I dunno."

"Maybe you better go down and thank Daddy and let him know you really wanna go. He feels bad. Would you do that for me?"

"I'll go fishing with him."

"But you better tell him. Will you do that for me?"

"I guess so."

"Good. Now go ahead and go down. I'll stay up here."

But she didn't. As I walked across the living room carpet, squinting in the light, I heard her come down the creaky stairs to stand at the bottom where she could listen unseen.

For a moment I stood at the side of the easy chair with my head down, squinting. "Dad?"

"Yeah?"

"Thanks. Thanks for taking me fishing."

He looked at me suspiciously for a moment, then slid his beer between his right thigh and the arm rest and spread his arms wide and I stepped forward and leaned over the arm rest so he could hug me. After releasing me, he said, "Good. We'll have a good time. Now you better get some sleep. We gotta get up early. Right?"

At the bottom of the stairs, Mom kissed me on the cheek as I passed, then whispered, "Thank you."

We began the two-hour drive before any hint of sunlight. At first, neither of us spoke, but as we crossed the bridge over the dark water of the canal and left Pendleton, he asked, "Why don't you go back to sleep?"

"I dunno. Not tired."

"No?"

"Not much."

As he drove he absently asked about school and talked a little about fishing and then his job. The moon was new and the houses were dense blurs passing by while in the dim green light of the speedometer and radio I played ticktacktoe on the steamy window. I noticed that the guy on the radio kept giving the time, and I wondered why anyone up so early or so late would want to be reminded every few minutes.

For a few dark miles, Dad was quiet again. Then I could feel him glance over at me as he began to repeat a family legend about his father. I straightened up on the seat and listened. It had been a long time since I had thought much about Grandpa Phillips, who in the opening of the story was standing in the middle of a plush office. Barley had a foreclosure notice crumpled in his fist and a fat lawyer was asking him to please sit down.

Barley went on standing.

I forgot about ticktacktoe.

Once more Barley explained that he had broken two ribs and bruised a lung in a construction accident, and that as soon as he finished healing and returned to work he would resume payments on the house. From what person, Barley asked once more, was he actually buying the house? Again the lawyer explained that he wasn't at liberty to reveal whose real estate he was managing; he regretted having to foreclose. Once more

Barley reminded the lawyer that he had eight children and nowhere else to live.

Perhaps the lawyer felt safe with an injured man because he stood up from the big polished wooden desk and broke the frozen politeness by telling Barley that he should have put away money for a time like this. Then he asked him to leave and not return without two months of mortgage payments.

Suddenly Barley was straddling the lawyer's chest, his callused hands squeezing the thick neck while the round face turned blue and the chubby arms and legs thrashed in the fine striped suit as the wide gasping mouth spittled out a name and address.

The next confrontation was with a butler, who informed Barley that Madam did not wish to be disturbed. Then she appeared, an elderly woman in a wheelchair, and asked what the problem might be. He removed his hat, stepped past the butler, and quietly explained. She had no idea, she said; of course he and his family could keep their home. She offered him a seat in the plush parlor, which he accepted, and directed the butler to push her to the telephone.

Before leaving, Barley asked, "And ma'am, how many children did you raise?"

Dad fell quiet as we waited at a red light on Route 78 in Depew with no other car in sight. When the light changed, he asked, "Did you understand?" Like my sixth-grade teacher who was always ruining a good story by asking the class what the moral was. I understood that the slow tortoise had beat the stupid hare, that the stupid writer hadn't told us whether it was the lady or the tiger behind the door, and that Grandpa had beat the crap out of a fat jerk. What more could there be to understand?

At dawn Dad parked at the Route 98 bridge between the small dairy and logging towns of Franklinville and Ischua. Carrying my fishing rod and some of the camping equipment, I followed him along the tracks that ran parallel to the creek, the stones of the railroad bed grinding under our steps. As the sun edged above a forested hill, we eased down the steep railroad bank. At the bottom we tossed our equipment over rusty barbed wire, then gingerly climbed over ourselves. We strode through the field of dewy wispy timothy to the winding stream bank where the mist rose and spilled over the shaded mud and unfurling ferns and up into the drooping branches and thin leaves of the wide willows.

Close to the creek the damp air was cold, and I wanted to keep moving, to explore and begin fishing. But Dad knelt down a few feet from the water and instructed me to do the same. "Learn from the water," he said. "Watch for trout. Watch and listen."

Upstream the creek swirled around a sharp bend and through the dark skeleton of a fallen willow and then rushed over a short shallow stretch of gravel and into the pool before us where it backed up briefly ahead of a glassy downstream bend. Just below the churning place where the fast water slipped under the clear water, the dorsal fins of trout sliced the surface without making a sound. "No splashes or bubbles. What that means is they're feeding on something a little under the surface. In what's called the film of the water. They could be taking insects that hatch out in the water before they fly off from the top—they're called emergers—but I haven't seen any on top or in the air. So I think they're taking pale evening duns that hatched last night."

"What's a pale evening dunce?"

"*Duns*—pale evening duns. Little yellow flies that hatch on the water when the sun goes down. So many it's hard to catch a fish with all the food on the water. But a lot of the duns die. A lot of them never hatch all the way or drown before they can fly off. I think the trout are still feeding on the dead ones."

I watched him remove the three lengths of bamboo rod from the aluminum case and screw on the reel and thread the line through the rod eyes and tie on a yellow fly so small that it didn't look as if it could fill the belly of a minnow. He squirted some type of liquid on the fly to make it sink faster and then crawled closer to the stream before getting up on his knees and beginning to cast, gracefully working the rod and line side to side and low over the misty water as he stripped off more line that finally straightened out about forty feet upstream. The fly settled on the fast water a little above the pool and quickly disappeared under the surface as it swept arching toward my father, who gradually lifted the tip of the rod and pulled in slack line linked somewhere to the fly hidden and moved by the water, and then suddenly he lifted higher and the rod bent under the weight of a trout. He stayed on his knees as he quickly landed it and broke its neck and slipped it yellow and brown and orange and quivering into his creel, which was stained dark with old blood. From that same pool he caught three more, and all but the smallest went broken-necked into the creel where later, as he fished upstream and the sun burned away the mist, the dead fish would be covered by a blanket of damp moss.

He fished upstream kneeling on the bank or crouching out in the current. I followed him for a while, learning where to cast, before I began to fish downstream with a spinning rod and small silvery spoon. I caught only one trout, a brightly colored brown. It was my first ever, and I called out to Dad, who was by then too far away to hear me over the sound of the water.

I had stopped fishing, and was sitting among ferns with my bare feet dangling in the cool water of Ischua Creek. My father stood back in the brush and watched me. I ticced contentedly. I was fixed on a broken limb of willow out in the current. Part of the limb was mired on the creek bottom, but the part above the water was bobbing, up and down and up and down, waving thin oval leaves. I was rocking back and forth and back and forth, my head bobbing and bobbing. I was utterly relaxed, at once on the shore and in the water, a branch and boy and stream.

"I don't care what that doctor says. You can't help it."

While scrambling to my feet I nearly fell into the creek.

"I didn't mean to scare you."

He was trying not to laugh.

"What?"

"I don't think you can help those habits of yours."

"I can. I can stop."

"Whadya catch?"

I held up my stringer.

"A nice trout. Good for you." Then he knelt and opened his creel and lifted the moss off the top layer of bright glistening fish.

We hiked back to the car for the rest of our supplies, then set up our canvas tent in the shade of the willows where we could hear the sound of the creek. We ate some of the food Mom had packed and then threaded thin branches through several of the gutted trout and roasted them over a small fire in a ring of stones. He said mine tasted the best.

After our nap in the tent, Dad began teaching me to fly cast. That evening, we roasted the remaining trout for dinner and talked until the sun was setting and temperature falling and out on the surface of the water the pale evening duns opened their new drying wings. Before they could fly off, some of them fell two or three times back to the water where the hungry trout rose to the rising and falling carpet. Dad went fishing again, but I was still sleepy and stayed behind, sitting on a rock close to the campfire. He caught only two even though he fished until he could no longer see the splashy rises or the bats that bumped his fly line as he cast in darkness not far from where I sat, warmed by the fire.

That night in my sleeping bag, a half mile from the nearest power line and seventy miles from the plant, I closed my eyes. The campfire crackled and popped and the water gurgled and somewhere in the darkness next to me my father talked about someday buying land and building a cabin in the hills above Ischua Creek.

A few days after the fishing trip, I discovered that I could bear to watch one of my tics. Reflected in the little mirror over the bathroom sink, my tongue slunk out of my mouth and over my upper lip, my head tipping back as if the tongue were a threatening serpent. I was seeing the tic as other children saw it. And when the tip of my tongue almost touched the end of my nose, I laughed.

During the week after I first saw and laughed at one of my tics, I occasionally repeated the experience with other tics. And as if easing back through the looking glass from a hellish wonderland, I gradually returned to the world of other children. Although sometimes my laughter was forced, I was learning to laugh with classmates and neighborhood children when they imitated my tics.

Eventually my peers gave up trying to anger and shame me.

And they had little choice. For on a bank of Ischua Creek, my father had already absolved me.

I asked if we could return to Ischua Creek. Dad was back to working overtime, and yawned and snarled a lot when he was home. He chewed his meat for another few seconds before he swallowed and answered, "Oh, I dunno. I doubt it, Mark. I gotta work Saturday and I'll be tired on Sunday."

"Oh, okay."

I knew better than to press him.

"And anyhow, the water'll be low now and it'll be a lot harder to catch fish."

Following supper, Mom called him into their bedroom, and after a while he came out and said to me in the living room where I was watching TV, "I don't see why we couldn't go on Sunday just for the morning."

On Sunday, she shook him awake in darkness. His eyes fluttered open and closed and then he resumed snoring. So she turned on the bright overhead light and went back to work on him, shaking his shoulders and calling to him as he tried desperately to sleep just a few more minutes. He was on his back and in the light he could see the blood in his closed eyelids. He believed a few more minutes would make a big difference. The hell with the expressway, the gate house, the locker room, the heat, the bending, the lifting, the molten metal, the dirt, the clean bosses in white shirts, the paycheck, the whole long day— just the hazy thought of it was exhausting. He had been dreaming about something pleasant and what he desired was a few more minutes. Just a few. But then she was talking about their son and fishing and he realized it was Sunday and mumbled something to her and made himself think about the steaming tea she would have waiting for him on the table. And then he began to long for a cigarette, and sat up squinting.

And perhaps as he attempted to stay awake and get out of bed he told himself that kids grow up fast and you never know what could happen before then.

You never know if you have much time left with them.

When we were halfway to Ischua Creek, I cracked open my window to let some of the smoke out into the predawn as the orange glow of the cigarette jabbed to and fro. On each side of the winding road, hills rose in the darkness beyond the gray meadows of the valley. Dad wasn't saying much; he was too tired. The radio announcer kept telling the time as if it were the most important thing in the world, and as the world whistled by I began to ask that habitual question of the traveling child: Are we almost there yet?

Are we almost there yet?

During the second night it sounds to Horace Guild as if the spring behind the lean-to is murmuring and swallowing watery words. He imagines he can detect the names of his wife and children, and though the names are quickly swallowed he is comforted and falls asleep.

Later he wakes to howls, and sits up for a long while with his musket on his lap while David snores. Then he adds wood to the dying fire and slips back into his bedding and tries to fill his mind with the thunk of axes and creaking crashing of timber and metallic jangle of wolf traps slung by chains over his shoulder and the baying of a hound and boom of his musket and thud of a limp cougar hitting the forest floor and the crunching crack of a deadfall on the back of a bear and the clink of metal on stone when a spade slices the head off a timber rattler. Yet somehow he can't imagine the forest and beasts vanquished; no matter how many trees and animals he imagines destroyed, they continue to haunt his fear like spirits.

The howling stops but it is almost dawn before he can again concentrate on the comforting murmuring of the spring. He listens and hears the name of his youngest daughter. He imagines the day they will move into a frame house of his own on cleared land, when she will ask, "Papa, how long will we live here?"

"Forever, sweetie. Forever."

The spring swallows, murmurs, and swallows, and he sleeps.

A Hard Row to Hoe

Whenever I see a photo or reproduction of *American Gothic,* I imagine that it is my mother's parents who are posing. And when the artist permits his models to take a break, Grandfather gooses Grandmother and she whacks him upside the head with the pitchfork handle and he laughs and laughs until they resume the pose that their marriage to the land has taken. Until I began spending weekends on their farm, about all that I knew of them was their pose: my grandfather as the living family legend who seldom took breaks from work except to shovel down mountainous helpings of food, and my grandmother as the bitter authoritarian.

Whenever my family ate dinner at the farm, I tried to keep up with him until ready to vomit, fearing the wiry glowering cook who wore her hair in a tight bun and gripped the thick handle of a black cast-iron frying pan. Yet Grandfather liked to talk and joke at mealtime despite her frequent admonitions. "Don't flap your gums with food in your mouth," she might say, or, "Shut your yap before your false teeth fly out." I was too afraid to laugh, but he poked fun at her and laughed at his own jokes, infuriating her all the more.

I was almost as surprised as my grandparents were when I first asked to spend a weekend on their farm. But there was good fishing in the nearby creek and I needed a break from the monotony of home, where Mom cleaned and cleaned, trying to make things right, and Dad was absent, away working at the plant and dreaming about owning a cabin in the Alleghenies. I needed a home away from home, and although my grandparents didn't realize it, they needed a break from their pose.

The legend of Grandfather Wagner begins in a small rented house in rural Michigan, where he was born. Later his father moved the family to western New York, and purchased a small farm. After graduating from the sixth grade, my grandfather quit school to help in the barn and fields. When he was eighteen, he moved out to become a sharecropper on a neighbor's farm. Soon he proposed to Nina Bartel, whose family spoke German at home, and eventually he had saved enough money to place a deposit on a small farm with two sides formed by swales and the others by Tonawanda Creek. His wife opposed his decision to buy, but her young role in the legend was still unimportant—and she held her tongue.

Every few years, the creek rose high enough to smother my grandmother's beloved gardens. While geese honked in the fiery blue sky, Grandmother planted seeds and potatoes and flower bulbs and worried about flooding. Grandfather took fish and muskrat and mink and ducks from the creek, but to her, Tonawanda Creek meant only mud and nettles and mosquitoes and, above all, a force that rendered all labor futile. When she was no longer a young and unimportant part of his legend, I heard her proclaim, "If I had it to do over again, I'd sure knock that farming idea out of Wagner's head." And after a brief pause she added, "And we sure wouldn't buy a place so foolish close to a creek."

He raised cattle and pigs and chickens and wheat and corn and oats and hay, cut and sold firewood, and labored for the highway department. And what did all that work get him, she demanded to know: "Here we are stuck on a muddy farm with all these stinking animals we can't leave for more than half a day and can't even grow a garden without the plants washed away or smothered by silt. Why doesn't the creek ever come up high enough to wash away the house and barn? Why does it just come up enough to kill my flowers?" The more she complained in life, the more she amused Grandfather; and the more he laughed, the angrier she got.

Often it seemed that Grandfather's entire life consisted of backbreaking work, inhaled food, and the shrug of laughter. He rose at 5 A.M. to do farm chores and to put in eight hours on state roads. As soon as he returned home from his state job, he pulled on black knee-high rubber boots and began his evening chores. Late in the evening he ate mashed or fried potatoes, boiled or fresh vegetables, meat fried in lard, fresh milk with a chunky layer of cream floating on top, bread and butter, pie, cookies, cake. And frequently, all during the meal, Grandmother nagged him to give up farming and demanded that they take a vacation and complained about the manure and mud he had tracked into the kitchen, while he shoveled in food and laughed as if it were silly madness to complain about a lifetime of hard labor and a little shit on the floor. After supper he watched television, laughing at the growling charlatan wrestlers or Lawrence Welk's corny jokes, but frequently, before a program was over, he climbed off the couch and stretched out on the floor, too tired to walk to the bedroom, and fell asleep. On the rare weekends when there was no planting, fertilizing, tilling, or harvesting to do, he cut, split, and stacked firewood to sell to the inhabitants of the nearby Tonawanda Indian Reservation.

When he had a hankering for fried or smoked fish, he went fishing in the creek. He dug up worms in the rich soil behind the chicken coop, dropping them into a coffee can half filled with leaves and dirt, and put on his straw hat and sprayed himself liberally with mosquito repellent. He fished with a ten-foot tapered tree branch, using bailing twine as line and baiting the sizable hook with three or four fat worms. When a fish took the bait, Grandfather leaned back and yanked the pole over his head, laughing maniacally as the fish smacked against the bank several feet behind him. To him, dinner was the sole purpose of fishing—and sometimes he dispensed with pole, hook, and line by placing an illegal trap in the creek.

Whenever I spent a weekend on the farm, I slept in one of the upstairs bedrooms. I fell asleep amid the odors of cedar closets and faintly musty quilts and woke early to the odor of coffee perking and of bacon, which in late autumn had been brined by Grandmother and smoked by Grandfather, frying in the big black skillet atop the combination propane and coal stove. While Grandmother continued to cook, I downed several thick slices of bacon, fried eggs, toast, a doughnut, and orange juice. Grandfather, who had already been up for two hours doing his morning chores, always tried to force more food into me with his standard warning: "Come on now! You'll never grow up, Markie, if you don't eat!" I always told him I didn't want to grow up, and he always laughed.

After breakfast I walked out to the pig pen where the big boar, crawling with flies and rubbing his bristly and mud-caked hide against a rough fencepost, waited for the table scraps I carried. He ate even the grease-saturated paper plate while the sows, piglets, and smaller boars stood back, watching and oinking and grunting and pawing. Then on my way to the barn I pulled up a clump of grass to feed to the black heifer who was so tame she could be ridden. In the barn, while my eyes adjusted to the dim light, I listened to the sloshing crunching of the chewing cattle, their heavy breathing, the spray of their urine, the plopping splat of their shit. The beasts eyed me, heads down, as I deeply breathed in the odors. Almost four decades later, whenever I pass a tractor and manure spreader on a highway, I roll down my car window.

After feeding the tame heifer, I climbed the steep stairs to the upper floor of the barn. From there I climbed the wooden ladder to the top of the wobbling haystack, where I studied hew marks on the roof beams and listened to the murmuring of pigeons and chirping of sparrows.

I abducted a black half-grown pigeon from a nest in the hay loft. I took him home in a shoe box. In the cellar, I kept him in a cage that Dad had constructed of wood-framed window screens, and fed him oats and wheat supplied by Grandfather. When Blackie was fully grown I took him outside and taught him to fly by throwing him into the air. He would wing to a row of small trees about three hundred feet from the house, then circle back to our yard. He usually landed on my head or on the back of Heidi, our gentle German shepherd.

One afternoon when I went to the cellar to feed Blackie, he was flopping on the floor of his cage. I decided that he must be dying of thirst, ran upstairs to the bathroom to fill his empty water dish, hurried back, and forced his head into the water—accidentally drowning him. When my mother later described the death of Blackie to Grandfather, he laughed long and hard.

When I was a little older and had a crush on one girl or another, I would study my grandparents to see where love might lead. To him love was a joke played on us, at which we might as well laugh while we could. To her love was a burden, a promise that could never be kept. It wasn't surprising, then, that the stubborn good humor of the man she loved irritated her so. She often called him stupid. He never countered by pointing out that he knew how to repair a tractor, raise a barn, bale hay, thrash oats, fell a tree, deliver a calf, butcher a hog. Instead he laughed.

Yet she loved the farm despite her venomous complaints. Once while we were on her porch watching the sun set behind the swampy woods, Grandmother recalled her alcoholic father with perplexity: "He must have been an awful man. As long back as I can remember and as young as I was, I hated to see him come home from work." And as young as I was, I recognized her statement about her father as a question: Was it him or me or everybody?

When she read the *Lockport Union-Sun and Journal* each evening, she began with the death notices and moved on to the police and court reports, the legal notices, and finally the wedding and birth announcements. She knew how many traffic tickets her second cousin and her postmaster's son and her neighbor's brother had received, and who had gone bankrupt or was an unwed mother or was on a second marriage or had been arrested. She clipped the articles and left them taped to her refrigerator for several days until moving them to the dinning room table. When the pile on the table had grown to about a dozen clippings, she filed them in boxes labeled "births" and "weddings" and "deaths" and "miscellaneous." If a visitor happened to ask about someone Grandmother knew, she might retrieve a clipping from the attic, read aloud any especially incriminating portion, and angrily identify the lost soul's weakness: "He drinks too much" or "is a dope fiend" or "never's been right in the head" or "grew up in a family of crooks" or "has a terrible bad temper." And then, voice calming, she would add, "Their baby died of meningitis" or "A tractor rolled over on him."

When the brother of her best friend killed himself, I was spending a weekend on the farm. In an old log cabin in an American concentration camp, the Tonawanda Indian Reservation, Charley Moses had lived with his sister, who telephoned grandmother minutes after the gun blast. Charlie had spent his days hunting and fishing in the swampy confinement of the reservation, and his nights drinking and fighting in bars owned by whites, perhaps feeling unconfined. Now he was dead, and over the phone, my grandmother asked Arlene, "Was he drunk?" Although I begged them to take me along to see a dead man with half his head gone, they ordered me to stay behind when they hurried out to their American Motors sedan.

The next morning, they returned to the reservation to clean Arlene's bloody and hairy parlor. I went fishing in the creek. When I returned to the yard dragging a stringer of rock bass and bullheads, Grandmother was kneeling on the lawn, her hands plunged in a pail of soapy water. I asked what she was doing and she said, "Trying to get brains off these curtains." She held up a splattered curtain and asked, "Who ever would have thought Charley Moses had so much brains?"

Arlene gave Charley's hunting rifle to Dad and his fishing tackle to me. Dad advertised the rifle in the classified section of the *Buffalo Evening News,* and as a potential buyer examined the weapon I spilled the story of the suicide. As the man was hurrying out of our house without making an offer, I added, "That gun sure does work." By the time Dad managed to sell the suicide weapon, I had spent two more weekends on the farm and had lost most of Charley's fishing hooks, sinkers, and lures on snags in Tonawanda Creek. And a few days after the sale, Grandmother served for Sunday breakfast a fried mixture of scrambled eggs and cow brains.

Burdened by the damning evidence stored in her attic and mind, my grandmother created her own earthly grace. She took down her hummingbird feeders early each August—"So they'll start south before the frost"—then drove to Agway to purchase several burlap sacks of seed for the birds that would winter on the farm.

On snowy mornings it was not unusual to see more than fifty birds at a time feeding where she had hung chunks of pork suet and scattered a bucket of seed, a simultaneously settling and rising blanket of sparrows and juncos and chickadees and jays and nuthatches and woodpeckers and grosbeaks. Her beloved cardinals were as striking as roses on the snow, and nothing angered her more than the killing of a cardinal by a hawk or stray cat. Predators altered the artificially reassuring scene she had created: food provided in stark January, innocent birds saved from nature, brightly colored life fluttering warm above the snow. The spell broken, she took possession of a fact and a shotgun, grimly waiting for a chance to kill the killer.

In spring the flock of cardinals dispersed to nest, and Grandmother was drawn, like the darting hummingbirds for which she was again providing sugar water, to the promise of flowers. Upon waking each morning in the blooming season, she fried an enormous breakfast for Grandfather and then, as habitually as some people drink their morning cup of coffee, limped through her flower gardens to absorb sweet odors as the iridescent blossoms opened to the rising sun. She returned to the kitchen, quickly ate a bowl of corn flakes, donned her straw hat, and then began her morning work in the gardens, her gnarled fingers pulling weeds and crushing pests so that beauty could bloom until the creek rose.

I had forgotten to pack the Hardy Boys mystery I had started at home. So from the shelf in the guest room, I picked out Joseph Wharton Lippincott's *The Wahoo Bobcat*. Even on a tepid night in May, the second-floor bedrooms were stuffy, and I opened the window before climbing into bed to read while the din of mating frogs and toads rose and fell like surf rolling in from the marshland on the fringe of the farm. Soon I became so immersed in the friendship between a farm boy and a wild bobcat that I didn't miss the Hardy Boys in the least.

I stayed up late before folding down the upper corner of a page and closing the book. As I turned out the light, I noticed a curtain of mosquitoes, drawn by light and hunger, probing for an opening in the window screens, and I soon fell asleep to the loud yearnings of frogs and toads and bugs.

I read the next morning until I heard Grandfather stomp into the house from the front porch, fling open the squeaky back door, and yell out to Grandmother, "Hey! It's break time. I want some coffee and doughnuts!"

Although it was second nature for her to battle him on several other fronts, she enjoyed keeping her man fed and was in the house by the time I'd dressed and descended the stairs. As I shuffled into the kitchen, she looked me over with one hand gripping an aluminum coffee pot and the other planted on her hip. "You just get up? Some farm boy—sleeping in till after nine."

"I been up. Reading."

"The Bible, I hope. You could use some Bible reading."

Grandfather laughed and said, "I'll bet he's got a girlie magazine up there."

"I'm reading a book."

"Be quiet. You'll be putting ideas in the boy's head."

"You better check under the mattress. I'll bet he's got a girlie magazine up there. Don't ya, Markie?"

"I should check under *our* mattress! Disgusting old billy goat!"

He slapped his thighs and threw back his head and roared, and I laughed along nervously. Then he changed the subject: "So Markie: going fishing?"

Instead I intended to explore the swales. He said I should take along a fishing pole anyhow, explaining that bullheads could be caught in openings where the water was too deep for cattails. But Grandmother warned that I would sink into quicksand or be smothered and sucked lifeless by millions of hungry mosquitoes. I insisted until she shrugged and said, "Then I guess I'll save some money on Christmas and birthday presents this year."

Grandfather had already inhaled his doughnuts and coffee and had departed before Grandmother finished frying my breakfast. While I tried to please her by forcing down too much food, she listened to the police scanner and during a lull in the action tuned in a radio to a news broadcast. The moon race had been in the news all year, and now, as we learned that an American rocket had lifted a dummy Apollo capsule into orbit, she asked, "Why would we want to go to such a godforsaken place as the moon?" Unlike my grandfather and father—both of whom dreamed of buying land in the hills and were avid followers of the moon race—she was already grounded on one godforsaken place.

Out on the lawn, she doused me with mosquito repellent. On my head she set a straw hat and to the rim taped a long stick of incense, which she lit, warning, "Mosquitoes don't like smoke, but don't let it burn down too much or your hat will catch on fire and you'll burn to death. And don't forget to make a walking stick so you can check for quicksand. And if you do make it back, don't forget to take off your muddy boots before you come in my house. How long do you think you'll be gone? I better call the Red Cross and tell them to have some blood ready for you."

I toted my BB gun into the swale for protection against the dangerous creatures—gators, tusked boars, poisonous snakes, armed rednecks—always lurking in the story I was reading. I knew such creatures were southern, but Lippincott's book still had me in its grip. The weather had been warm, and you never could tell how far north a beast or redneck might migrate in search of prey or moonshine.

On mushy ground, I hiked the fringes of the swale, periodically deafened by the flocks of redwing blackbirds feeding and mating and simultaneously rising and landing, as if some screeching god were shaking an enormous black and red quilt. At first I could see neither over nor past the tall and thick cattails, but eventually the ring of growth thinned enough for me to spot a pool of water splotched with lily pads. Bullfrogs rested on some of the thin green pads. In the middle of the pool muskrats had heaped up a house of cattails and swamp grass, and atop it were the claws and scattered shells of crawfish eaten by mink. Beneath the cloudy sky the screeching of the flocks seemed a fittingly tumultuous background to a scene where, as Lippincott put it in his book, "someone was constantly trying to eat someone else." Yet the only danger to myself I had encountered was the thickening cloud of mosquitoes that followed and swirled around me like a gathering tornado.

I needed to get closer to the open water before I could fish, but I had forgotten to bring a walking stick and so pushed through the cattails with tentative steps. At the edge of the water I set down my gun and baited my hook with a worm, but then, as I was about to cast, the soft ground gave way with a slurp and I slid feet first and on my back into the brackish swale. I jumped up coughing and gasping and cursing. The water was barely two feet deep but the incense had been extinguished, and instead of insect repellent I was covered with fetid muck.

Grandmother heard my scream. She saw me burst out of the cattails and sprint to higher ground in a plowed field as I waved the fishing pole and BB gun over my head like a pair of machetes, fighting the smothering cloud of mosquitoes drilling me in a hundred places. As I crossed the field, I jettisoned the useless gun and began beating myself half senseless with the freed hand as I ran. Later she told me that I had reminded her of a horror movie she had seen about soul-snatching zombies that rose up at night from the bottom of a lagoon. Except the mucky zombies didn't run for their lives and scream and beat themselves.

She was still laughing when she met me on the front stoop. "Don't even think for a second you're going into my house covered with muck. Strip down to your underwear. I'll get the hose."

As I departed the farm after Sunday dinner, my grandparents stood together on the edge of the gravel driveway watching my overfed family squeeze groaning into Dad's new Volkswagen. Grandfather wore denim coveralls and Grandmother a long denim dress and a white apron. She was clutching the handle of a broom held upside down at her side. He said, "Come back soon, Markie. You better come back next weekend, don't you think so?"

"He will," she said. "I should say so. Yes."

The Allegheny spring consumes winter slowly, a sun-warmed snake swallowing a cold frog. The nights are starry and yet freezing when the afternoons become blinding, the bright covering of the land hopping with snow fleas, and men drill sugar maples and drive spiles and hang buckets or string plastic tubing from tree to tree. They fire up the evaporators in the sugar shacks, and passerbys are relieved to see steam billowing like smoke signals announcing the flowing of the sap. The short sugaring season ends when the swelling buds absorb the watery sweetness, the maples blooming, infusing the hills with scarlet—like blood pulsing beneath a thin membrane. Then in the half-light of clear windless dawns, the gobbles of wild turkeys ring from hilltops, and in May the gobbling becomes higher pitched and more frantic as the hens disappear to sit on eggs, and the scarlet of the hills becomes a green and white haze as leaves open and dogwoods bloom in scattered white puffs. By the middle of the month, farmers walk from house to barn and are surprised to see that on the surrounding hillsides the trees are almost fully leafed, as if during the warm rainy night the mounting green had burst a dam and welled over the land.

Grandfather and Dad had made a decision to look at and perhaps buy some land in the newly green Alleghenies. Just before kissing her husband good-bye in the driveway, Grandmother said, "You two don't need any more land to take care of than you already got. Wagner, you got more than you can handle now, and Jim, I'll bet you haven't even mowed your lawn yet this weekend. Who's gonna do it, Eva and little April? Well, I hope you two don't think me and Eva are gonna come down and cook for a bunch of drunken filthy hunters—because we ain't. You're on your own. Land drunk and foolish." As Grandfather drove out the driveway, she hollered after us, "Land! Land is what we get buried in."

As the old pickup bounced and rattled southward over the washboard roads of the Tonawanda Indian Reservation, Dad said, "Do you think she'll change her mind, George, and come along when it's hunting season?"

"Oh, God. I'd sell the cabin the next day."

Grandfather didn't believe in main roads and seldom used a map. On his dashboard he had mounted a compass, which often urged us in a direction that the back roads didn't run. He was forever stopping at small gravelly intersections and turning corners or back from dead ends. On the rough back roads I bounced like a doll on the springy seat and spent most of the journey with my eyes closed in a cold creepy fog of motion sickness as the men talked and laughed somewhere in the irritating background. Occasionally I mumbled, "Are we almost there yet?"

"George doesn't know where the hell we are."

"Go to sleep, Markie. When you wake up we'll be there."

And so it was: somehow I fell asleep and when I woke from a dream the truck engine was bucking and backfiring to a halt on a dirt road in the Alleghenies. We were several miles from Wellsville, an oil town gone bust in the shadow of steep hills near the Pennsylvania border. Someone was selling a small cabin and several acres of hardwoods. Dad was thinking about going halves with Grandfather. I was plucked at dawn and brought along to keep my mother's Sunday bearable.

I was amazed by the great difference between this woods in early June and the forest in the state park where Dad had taken me deer hunting in November. It wasn't just the thick canopy and lack of snow, but also the sudden dimness and the rich green and brown odors of growth and decay, and the birdsongs that lost the shrillness they possessed in open spaces, becoming more earthy, and the slugs and snails and bugs and salamanders and tree frogs that I kept pointing out to the men, who couldn't have cared less. They were examining deer trails and discussing which maples and oaks and ash and cherry could be selectively logged to help pay for the land. Even on a steep downward slope we couldn't see far because of the leafy maple and beech saplings waiting for the parent trees to die or be blown over or cut down, waiting for their years in the light, and Grandfather kept checking his compass. We zigged and we zagged. I was so engrossed in the life I was spotting on the dead leaves beneath the ferns that my stomach calmed until Grandfather caused me to jump by exclaiming, "Look!" He strode up to a beech with shredded bark. "You see that, Jim?" He ran his hands over the damage. "A bear did that. Climbing it to eat the nuts. A bear did that."

"No shit? A bear?"

"A bear. Sure as shit. A goddamn bear."

I asked, "Is it still around?"

Grandfather laughed. "Afraid he might be hungry, Markie?"

Dad touched the tree. "Look at that, Mark. A bear was here."

Despite the ramshackle cabin, my father was ready to buy until they finally located the spring that the seller had described to Grandfather with a good deal of exaggeration. For several feet around a mossy log, the ground was mushy, but after Dad dug into the earth with a stick, the water trickled slowly and brown into the little trench. "I don't know, George. It's only early June and the weather isn't dry yet. I'll bet this spot is bone dry by the middle of July."

"Then we'll just have to carry water in. Or dig a well."

"I don't know, George."

I could tell that my father had lost interest, but felt certain my grandfather would buy. As we stepped out onto the shoulder of the dirt road where the truck was parked, he said, "I haven't seen a bear since I was a boy up in Michigan. Yep, it's good to see bear sign again." As he reached into a coverall pocket for the truck key, he turned around to look back into the woods.

On Saturday when Grandfather returned to the Allegheny property to deliver a down deposit to the seller of ursine bless-

ings, Grandmother and I stayed back on the farm to spread—
and as it turned out, to search through—a truckload of rich topsoil that had been delivered for use in her flower gardens.

While filling a wheelbarrow, she noticed a flint arrowhead
atop a shovelful of the soil. She hurried back into the house
with her black and gray prize, flawlessly knapped and honed
and still sharp. She climbed the steep stairs to the hot attic to
rummage through crammed cardboard boxes for a saved
newspaper clipping about local Indian artifacts. By com-
paring the arrowhead to the descriptions in the article, she
determined that the flint had been crafted by the Hopewell
Indians, who had dotted the western New York landscape
with mysterious earthen mounds long before the arrival of
Europeans.

She returned to the garden with the yellowed clipping
slipped folded into the breast pocket of her coveralls, in case we
were to find more artifacts. Although I was eager to find an arrowhead, it was Grandmother who found several more, thrusting each into my face like an ancient truism: "There! Another
one!" And once she added, "The newspaper said they don't
know much about them. Don't know what they believed or
their words or anything else. Just they're gone. They must've
been heathens, though—just like all the rest. Believed in spirits.
Worshiped nature and all that heathen stuff. Well, so look at the
good it did them."

Each time she unearthed another, she hobbled over to the
hose to wash off the soil with muddy water pumped from
Tonawanda Creek. Then in sunshine and human hands, for the
first time in a thousand years, the killing tool glinted.

━━►◆◄━━

Now that Horace and David and their older boys are felling the trees that shade the narrow stream, the trout have become fewer. Yet only passenger pigeons are more plentiful than brook trout, and where the immense flocks roost in beech stands and feed on the nuts, a man can kill enough—a dozen with each load of shot—to feed his family and hogs all autumn. During the warmer months, there is ample game despite the wolves that Horace catches in iron traps and earthen pits to collect the bounty, and he has come to like the taste of venison and bear better than mutton and pork, if not beef. He enjoys hunting and trapping and fishing far more than clearing and cultivating fields.

He likes the life of a predator so much that he rides his horse twenty-five miles to the new town of Scio, where a double bounty is offered on a black three-legged wolf. For two weeks, he pursues that dark crippled phantom through the surrounding forest. Unable to run down deer, it feeds on the livestock and poultry of the beings whose trap cost it a leg. Men track it through deep snow, pursue it with hounds, set traps and snares and carefully cover pits and poison the carcasses of sheep, but neither Horace nor anyone else collects the bounty. For many years after the normal lifespan of a wolf, the black wolf is rumored to be killing sheep and calves and chickens for a hundred miles around. And by then it seems to Horace that men must be longing for evidence of some kind of life that cannot be killed.

A Map of Forever

After working ten-hour shifts and Saturdays for three weeks in a row, everything about his job, even his buddies, had become nearly unbearable to my father. He began to eat his lunch alone in the fresh brightness behind the Water Intake Building, where he sat and watched the water-skiers leaning back in the sunshine and wind on the blue river just as he and my mother had on their vacation four years earlier. On a Saturday afternoon, one of the plant supervisors swung past in a new speedboat. My father waved back. Then he finished his lunch, wiped his lips with a napkin, snapped shut his lunch box, and crawled—"just because I felt like doing it"— out onto the breakwall that squared off the water outside the building. Far out on the iron wall, only twelve inches in width at the top, he stood up in the full breeze and sunshine like a skier, and for an instant lost his balance above the water that was sucked violently into the plant. He was still shaken when he came home that night. "I almost fell off the breakwall today," he said, standing in the middle of our kitchen. "Accidentally."

On evenings when he was home for our family supper, he appraised us kids with a red glare and we pretended to like our lima beans and squash. Gone for now were the occasional mealtimes when he told us about his welding feats and the boss who kept asking him to let the company pay his way through engineering school and the history and marvels of coal and union struggles and the joyful or sorrowful stories about his fellow workers and their families.

One evening he broke the intensifying quiet by telling us in a matter-of-fact tone—while spearing with his fork the extra pork chop I coveted—that he had bloodied the mouth of a fellow worker who had somehow given insult. And a few days later, he came home from work early and announced that he had ended an argument with a foreman by quitting his job. When later that evening the foreman called our house, Mom was greatly relieved to hear Dad accept the apology. A decade earlier, my Uncle Al had been a welder at the power plant and had told a foreman to take a flaming acetylene and oxygen enema. When that foreman had called to apologize, Al had instructed him to "stick your sorry up your same sorry ass where I already told you to stick my sorry job."

Rather than quit, Dad refused overtime for two weeks, and in his spare time planted a large vegetable garden between the garage and orchard. From a retired grape grower he bought a little red Farmall tractor with a plow and disc and worked on our side yard as if it were the lower forty. Grandfather delivered a truckload of manure and a few bales of straw, but warned that it was too late in the year to be planting a vegetable garden. Dad replied cryptically, "Everything is late, George. Everything is always too damn late."

As he nursed his garden all that summer, he reminded me of Grandmother. He always checked on his plants before leaving for work and soon after arriving home in the evenings. I watched him almost lovingly sprinkle pesticide powder on his tomato plants and was reminded of Mom sprinkling talcum powder on April when she was an infant. Mealtimes became more relaxed and conversational and, as if he had merely needed the diversion of a garden, stayed that way for a few weeks after he resumed working overtime at the power plant.

Dad was bothered by more than his job.

While driving home from work he sometimes tried to understand the antiwar protests and free love and flag burning and marijuana and LSD so much in the news. Sometimes he tuned the radio into what the kids called music: "Day Tripper" by the Beatles or perhaps Barry McGuire's "Eve of Destruction." But he felt he was being insulted because he loved his country and cut his hair and didn't use drugs and worked his ass off like the fathers of the college kids who were smoking pot and taking over the dean's office. He was part of the generation that had barely survived the threat of Nazi and Japanese foremen in charge of us all, and now it seemed to him and many other blue-collar workers that these kids wanted to hand America over to Communist foremen. His passionate take on current events led me to write a letter to one of the Buffalo newspapers in which I defended American involvement in Vietnam. For a few weeks my father was proud of his patriotic and published son, even though I wanted to grow my hair longer.

During the turmoil of the 1960s, he frantically told me everything he knew about coal. The gardening man who was as infatuated as Ponce de León with the water of springs was equally obsessed with hard coal ripped from the American earth. "Electricity," he often said with curious pride, "is just inefficient coal." Yet he longed for pure water and green hills where he could forget about coal.

Back when he was newly employed by the power plant, he signed out of a public library a book about electricity and another about coal, thinking he might learn something that would help him to be promoted. But after finishing the book about coal he returned the other unread and signed out more about coal. From then on he read every newspaper and magazine article he came across on the subject of coal or coal mining. Whenever the news reported a mine disaster or strike, he barked, "Be quiet!"—whether or not any of us happened to be talking—and turned up the sound.

As the 1960s grew more tumultuous, coal somehow became linked to Dad's desire to keep me nearly bald. He liked to say that the only way he could tell the long-haired boys from the long-haired girls on the college campuses was that "the girls are the ones not wearing bras." As college students chanted and waved protest signs, he shut off the news and ordered me onto a step stool in the kitchen. Nearly shouting to be heard above the buzz of the hair clipper, he would talk coal.

He explained that coal was formed from "ferns as tall as trees": plants that died and were covered by other fallen ferns, then by shallow seas and deepening sediment. The weight and pressure and heat transformed the plant matter into hardening blackness as dinosaurs and mastodons came and went, as apes evolved into men and men learned to use fire, began to farm, invented alphabets and the wheel.

He explained that after people cut down all the trees around their towns they began to burn the strange black rocks that could be found near the surface of the earth. Eventually they used coal to replace charcoal in the making of coke and to power the factories of the Industrial Age, which were built near mines. The black veins were excavated deeper and deeper, the air above the clustered factory towns became almost as dark as the entrances to the mines, and every building and every street and inch of ground was layered with deepening fly ash, gardens dying, children coughing up ashy mucous speckled with blood, families sweltering in houses with windows shut tight against the filth.

And then men used coal to fire steam locomotives that pulled long earth-rumbling carloads of coal to factories and eventually to the new power and steel plants built many miles from the mines. In America, where coal was plentiful, homes were lit by electricity, and steel skyscrapers rose like thousands of towers of Babel. In the deep Appalachian and western mines, Irish and German immigrants and the sons of emancipated slaves worked on their hands and knees up to sixteen hours per day. They labored in black water and stale dusty air, by the light of their miner's lamps, surrounded by their shit and piss and listening to the rolling cracking of the low ceilings, fighting off enormous mine rats at lunchtime. Their sons, not yet thirteen years old, worked above ground in dim dusty rooms picking slate off conveyors.

The wives and daughters tried without running water to keep babies healthy and a small drafty shack clean of coal dust in the company town where the proprietor of the mine owned the shacks and the stores and charged so much for rent and food and paid so little in script that there was no escaping. In the company town, if the miner did not first die in a cave-in or flood or explosion, he would almost certainly die of "natural causes"

well before he was old, of black lung or pneumonia or lung cancer or tuberculosis, coughing up coal-speckled blood. And one
after the other, his sons would descend into the blackness, slate
pickers no more.

Exasperated by one of Dad's dark tales and squirming on
the chair while he talked loudly over the buzz of the clipper, I
reminded him of the time that his union was planning to strike
and he had smuggled home in his lunch box a part from plant
machinery that he had sabotaged. I asked, "So why didn't the
miners do something? Why didn't they strike or something?"

It was a question he had been waiting for. "Why didn't they
do something?" He shut off the clippers. "You mean grow their
hair long like girls and take dope and boycott the classes their
fathers worked to pay for? Why didn't they do something? Why
didn't they *do* something? Well, go get me a Genny. And then
I'm gonna tell you what they did."

I fetched his mug, rinsed it with tap water, and removed a
bottle from the case of Genesee on the porch. He sat down in a
chair at the kitchen table, where he accepted the bottle and mug,
lit his pipe, and began to tell—while he poured and puffed,
foam rising, smoke filling the air—about the coal miners' fight
with John D. Rockefeller.

In the rain and snow of late September, the miners struck,
abandoning the mines and the company-owned shacks. With the
children dressed in rags and the furniture piled on wagons or
carts that the mining families pushed without the aid of horses,
the families gathered, exposed to prairie winds, in tent towns set
up by the United Mine Workers of America. Gunfights became
continual between the company guards and strikers, and National Guard troops, although sent by the governor of Colorado

as peacekeepers, joined the company guards in strafing tents full of women and children. By spring, when President Wilson sent in the army to restore peace, scores of people had been killed. Six months later, with the union out of money and the children of miners starving, with another winter howling out of the mountains and hurling across the prairie, the union called off the strike.

Dad paused to sip beer, then asked, "And what do you suppose the average miner gets paid per hour these days?" He might as well have asked any of several other questions that were closer to his point: Don't we have our own home? Don't we have running water and electricity? Don't you have a father who earns enough money to put food on the table and clothes on your back and then some? Don't you have a father who started out as a sweeper and ended up a welder? Does the government still gun down the families of striking workers? Do you have to pick slate all day? Hasn't this country come a long way? Is there a better country? Well, then, why do you want to grow your hair long like those Commie students who are trying to tear down everything that the American working man has fought for and sacrificed for and built from the ground up?

One evening when Kim and I were helping him weed his garden, he asked, "Kim, where does coal come from?"

"Coal?" She shrugged. "From the ground?"

"Nope." He looked at me: "Mark?"

I stood up with mock pride. Unlike Kim, I'd been through this before. For effect I paused and scratched my buzzed head. Then I answered, "From the bowels of the earth."

He jumped up. "That's right! From the bowels of the earth! That's exactly right! From the bowels of the earth!" Grinning, he kicked the ground, scattering straw and loose soil over several radish plants. "You hear that, Kim? From the bowels of the earth."

Every so often in town we passed some gentleman wearing a freshly pressed two-hundred-dollar suit and a sparkling gold watch and gleaming leather shoes. Dad would spit on the sidewalk and mutter, "You son of a bitch."

The first few times I witnessed this, I assumed my father had recognized someone who had wronged him, but I was so frightened by his sudden anger that I didn't ask questions. Eventually, though, I realized that he was spitting and cursing at generic executives, bankers, politicians, lawyers. I realized that he hated the rich as much as he hated the antiwar protesters. Or as he once put it, "I'd like to see those kids come in the plant and try to tell the guys I work with how oppressed we are." He added, "And in another ten or fifteen years, who do you think will be the politicians and fat bankers and crook lawyers and big businessmen defending the almighty way things are? Well, I'll tell you who. It'll be those kids who are out there waving Communist flags."

Communism, to him, was a government under which the bankers and lawyers and politicians and executives owned everything and possessed total power. The difference in America was that the working man at least had a fighting chance.

I had geography homework concerning the Allegheny Plateau and so spread out on the kitchen table one of Dad's creased, wrinkled, and torn maps of southwestern New York. I didn't find the answers I was seeking but spent a long time examining the myriad routes he had traced over the glacial hills and valleys as he had scoured the Alleghenies for land and springs. It was the map of a treasure hunter and a fugitive, a map worthy of a pioneer. A few years later, when I was a junior in high school, my English teacher unknowingly led me to some understanding of my father by assigning a patriotic essay: "The map of America," Archibald MacLeish would explain to me in the essay, "is a map of endlessness, of opening out, of forever and ever."

I hated those scalpings. I was desperately in love with a girl and hoped to become more attractive by growing my hair longer like other boys. But if I so much as mentioned longer hair, Dad would fire up the clipper and order me onto the step stool. It was like climbing into Old Sparky, the state's electric chair. I also began to hate those stories about coal, and perhaps more than that.

One morning he walked out of the house trailing the statement, "I'm giving you a haircut tonight."

When he was out of earshot, I announced, "I hate him. I hope he dies."

Mom spun from the sink and started toward me with sudsy fists, but stopped herself halfway across the kitchen. Sitting across the table from me, Kim began to cry. Mom returned to the sink, resumed washing dishes, and said quietly, "Well, tough shit, buddy."

Peggy was skinny and wore glasses and was taller than I. I loved her because sometimes she acted as if she loved me.

I loved her teasing and glances and giggles, her flattering reflection of an image that I otherwise found wanting. We were in love all year but didn't go on a single date.

Boys were growing longer hair and were wearing tight white jeans and penny loafers and almost any color socks except white. Meanwhile, the principal of my school, standing on an island where the calendars said it was 1950, was sandbagging the 1960s. Clutching a ruler, bald Mr. Keech waited at the main entrance each morning as we students streamed in from the buses: a girl's skirt could be only so far above her knees, a boy's hair only so far over the tops of his ears. But how do you judge objectively whether pants are too tight? You slip an egg between the boy's pants and his waist, and if the shell cracks, the pants are too tight.

Mr. Keech never needed to measure my hair or check the fit of my pants. Whenever my hair began to lay down, Dad got out the clippers. And when Mom took me clothes shopping, tight anything was out of the question: I was supposed to grow into my clothes. The nearest I got to wearing tight white jeans was white socks. I did get to wear penny loafers, but they were plastic.

During school dances I sat glued to the gymnasium bleachers with the other eighth-grade dorks. We watched girls dance with each other or with boys who had to keep brushing hair out of their eyes and who, when the dancing got wild, kicked off their leather penny loafers. I didn't mind my shortness, enjoyed popping my pimples, and had learned to laugh at my tics. But to be attired like a refugee from a 1950s sock hop and to have my head shaven like a convict's felt like going naked in public. I believed that somehow my preventable freakishness denoted guilt. That four-eyed Peggy wasn't exactly Miss America didn't lessen my insecurity. What if I asked her to dance and she said no? I might kill myself. Or my parents.

One afternoon during gym class, Peggy and another girl snuck away from field hockey to watch the boys perform broad jumps near the track. I was passionately determined when it was my turn to leap. Watching me was the broad I wanted to jump.

I sprinted to the board and leapt farther than I had ever before, and as gravity pulled me back toward earth, I lifted my legs parallel to the ground, gaining a few more lateral inches. But when I landed on my ass and on my hands opened at my sides, I felt my left forearm turn quickly and fluidly at the elbow as if it were a greased bolt spun easily by a wrench. I felt no pain until I stood up and saw, pressing against the stretched skin, the distinct outline of my dislocated joint. The hospital tests would show that I also had chipped and cracked the radial bone and had torn cartilage.

I decided I would moan and groan and complain about pain in my elbow. Then standing before Dad in faked agony, my arm still in the cast, I would ask him if I could please grow my hair a little longer. But that evening I had to change my plans after a black stranger walked into my home without knocking. Even his lips were black. Only his reddened eyes were not black. After laughing at my frightened failure to recognize him, he explained that he had been welding in a bad place and that the showers at the power plant were shut down for repairs.

I couldn't work up the nerve again until the next evening, when he came home clean. He was sitting in his easy chair with his eyes half-closed, drinking beer and watching TV, and I was sitting hunched forward on the couch, moaning and groaning and rubbing the cast with my right hand. Wearing a grimace, I finally stood up during a commercial and crossed the carpet to the easy chair, and then asked in a pained voice, "Dad, won't you please let me grow my hair out a little longer than this?"

And he didn't even look away from the television as he said, "I don't give a shit."

Dad hadn't been offered overtime for nearly two weeks. He and Mom were sitting on the couch with April between them, and he was walking two fingers up April's leg: "Squeak mouse, squeak mouse, coming to April's house!"

As the fingers reached her stomach, she shrieked and laughed while writhing, then pushed away his hand and covered up her abdomen. He grinned and leaned down to kiss the top of her head. Then he looked over at Mom. "You know, Eva, I still say it would be good for these kids if we had a cabin and some land. We'd all have a lot of fun. Wouldn't you guys like a pond to swim in?"

I said nothing.

Kim asked, "Can we just buy a pool?"

Mom said, "I think I'll change the channel."

Later when I went out to the kitchen to make hot cocoa, he was hunched over one of his maps. The table was cluttered with his unlit pipe, a silvery pouch of tobacco, a pack of L&M cigarettes, a clear ashtray, a brown empty beer bottle, the classified section of the newspaper, and the worn map on which he was tracing another route as he smoked a cigarette. I poured milk into the pan and dumped in several heaping spoonfuls of Nestlé

Quick and stood with my back to him, stirring the dark soup as it heated over the blue flame. When it was steaming I noisily sipped some from the spoon, burning my lips. Not enough chocolate. I added another big heap, poured what would fit into a mug, and headed for the living room.

"Wanna go fishing Sunday?" he asked.

I wanted to drink my delicious steaming cocoa. "I thought the streams were low this time of year."

"A buddy from work is renting a cottage on Cuba Lake down that way. We'll fish in the lake. Catch some perch. Maybe some walleye. He's got a boat." Then he paused until he was sure the coast was clear before he added, quietly, "Maybe we'll look at some land while we're down there."

He had been making occasional trips into the Alleghenies on Sundays, supposedly to go fishing, but he never brought home any fish. It had been weeks since he had asked me to go along, and Mom had taken to joking nervously about his "Sunday girl-friend."

It was risky to say no outright, so I said, "I got a big test on Monday."

"It'll give you something to do in the car."

I shrugged and said, "I guess."

He looked down at his map, and I fled with my delicious steaming cocoa.

He eased up on the gas as the highway began to straighten through the narrowing valley. There the last glacier had ceased its southern slide, and the unshorn land, rising above the valley beyond the shimmering twists of Ischua Creek, thrust higher

and steeper. We had barely spoken at all since leaving Pendleton, though now he told me about the last glacier. "I say here's
where the Alleghenies begin. In the encyclopedia at home it
says they go up through Pennsylvania to the New York border,
like mountains need a building permit or something. On the
map it looks like they go even farther than this into New York.
But I say this is the spot. Imagine that ice? Huh? High as clouds.
Cutting the tops off mountains. Can you imagine that ice?"

I didn't reply. The boys in the neighborhood had planned a big
football game, and football was the only sport I was good at. The
heck with glaciers. I wanted to be back home breaking tackles.

The forested hills seemed to wake him fully for the first time
that day. He continued to talk about the land, one rough hand
on the wheel and the other gesturing as his head turned from
side to side. He told me that before the Alleghenies were settled,
the virgin forest was mostly maple and beech and birch and
ironwood, hardwoods that can grow in the dense shade of older
trees. But hemlock clutched the steepest hillsides, and white
pine sprung up where wind or fire had swept away the hardwoods. When they were cut, some of the hemlock were five
hundred years old, and some of the pine two hundred feet tall.
"A squirrel could go a thousand miles without ever coming
within a hundred feet of the ground."

As my father talked about the animals of the great forest, his
tone annoyed me: he sounded a little like our minister reciting a
long prayer. "Bear and cougar and wolves lived in the woods.
Every stream so full of brook trout that a man could catch them
with his bare hands. Huge flocks of turkeys. Passenger pigeons
flew over in flocks five miles wide and ten miles long. They
darkened the valleys, blocked out the sky."

I felt obliged to give an amen: "Grandfather told me there were rattlesnakes."

"Yep. Timber rattlers. Elk, too, in this area."

I couldn't recall the difference between elk and reindeer, and didn't ask. In his reverent tone, Dad went on talking about the animals of the great vanquished forest. Trying to quiet him, I said, "Well, they're gone for good now."

"Don't be so sure. The grouse and deer were almost extinct fifty years ago, and now look. They're all over. Ischua Creek's full of trout. Even the bear and turkey are starting to come back. Down in Pennsylvania they're releasing elk again. Fifty years ago, the woods were almost gone. But then the farms started going belly up because of the bigger ones out West. Now look. Hell—I've been lost in the woods around here. More than once, too."

I began to notice how many barns were abandoned and sagging, the silos down and the surrounding fields grown up with brush and saplings. Even some of the old houses were uninhabited, the windows broken and the clapboards weathered bare. In weedy yards, lilacs grew wild, and where corn and oats had once bent in the wind, deer fed on acorns under the cover of young trees. Beyond the valleys and gentler hillsides, up where the land had always been too steep and thin for farming, the forest became taller. I could picture a bear up there shredding a rotten log in a tangled windfall, licking up plump white grubs while jays scolded from the treetops.

Then I was picturing myself back in Pendleton, scoring a touchdown to the cheers of my team.

Before turning onto the back road that would take us over the hills to Cuba Lake, Dad gassed up at Cookie's store in the eye-blink town of Ischua. Out on the oily gravel between the car and single pump, he paid for the gas and asked Cookie if he knew of any land for sale by the owner instead of a real estate company. Cookie replied that he couldn't think of any offhand. "But come on, maybe somebody else does."

"Dad. Can I get a candy bar?"

Inside the small store, five old men in lawn chairs were smoking cigarettes and pipes between the short counter and the few shelves crammed with canned goods. Cookie said, "This here fella from Buffalo—"

"Pendleton. Twenty miles from Buffalo—a different county even. Closer to Lockport."

"Fella from Buffalo here wants to buy land for sale by the owner. Wants to build a cabin like the rest from Buffalo. I don't know, though. Can't think of any offhand."

After a few more puffs, one of the men pulled the pipe stem from his mouth, just barely, and said, "Maybe he should talk to Brown. Been saying for years he's gonna break up the farm and sell." Then the man looked at the city fella for the first time, and said with faint taut grief, "Worth a try, Brown is. Not far."

In dirty green knee-high rubber boots, the farmer stood outside the barn on the dry cracked shit. He was trying to shoe away the flies with his red, white, and blue Agway cap as he gazed over the barbed wire fence and down the sloping field of thin hay that needed mowing.

The mere thought of mowing and raking and baling and stacking made him tired. It was nine in the morning and he hadn't milked yet. The thought of milking made him tired, too. Maybe this would be the last year. Old dairy farmers such as himself were dividing their increasingly unprofitable farms into forty- or fifty-acre plots and selling to city men who wanted to build cabins and ponds and booze away the deer season. Maybe this was the year he would sell; the right guy comes along, he'd start selling off.

Saplings of poplar and cherry and oak and ash and maple would push up through the goldenrod and blackberry briars where he had once plowed and disked the land, and those that weren't chewed down by the deer would grow into trees. Then in their shade the beech and ironwood and birch and more maple would come up; he supposed it wouldn't be long before the land was as wild as when some pioneer was chopping down his first tree. And he didn't give a damn. Sell out, buy a place in town, kick his feet up before he died, maybe get drunk and go hunting. Why should the city fellas have all the fun? The hay would be straw if he didn't cut it soon and the bursting cows were bawling in their stalls and the goddamn flies were already biting and it was gonna be a hot sticky day, and he was tired.

After an interminable conversation with the farmer out in the sun behind the barn, Dad returned to the car and said, "Jesus Christ. Flies about ate me alive."

He drove a short ways back down the narrow dirt road, then parked half on the road and half on the weedy shoulder. After climbing over a rusty and leaning barbed wire fence, we crossed a pasture to an acre stand of white pine. In the middle of the thick pines we found an old hollow ash and up between its roots rose water. The clear water slipped downhill over gravel and around mossy stones. On his dampened hands and knees, head lowered like a silent thirsty deer, my father was surprised at the quick painful stab of the cold as he drank.

"Ice!"

He was grinning.

Since the rest of the property was nearly treeless, I asked where he intended to hunt if he bought it.

"You can plant trees, but you can't plant water."

He held my hand in the water until I complained that my head ached.

Then he sat down on a thick arching root of the ash. "This spring," he said, "is what I've been looking for. This spring will supply all our drinking water. This will be our refrigeration system. This will fill the trout pond I'm gonna have built. And over there," he added, pointing through the pines, "will be where we'll build our cabin. A stone fireplace. Bunk beds. Propane lights and stove." He stood up. "And absolutely no goddamn power company electric!" Then he brushed his right hand, damp and cool, over my brushcut. "Yep, Mark, we're gonna have lots of good times here."

We stood quietly looking out through the trees at the place where he had already decided to build his cabin, and I wondered how many touchdowns I would have scored.

Dad skipped his shower after work so that he could get to the bank in Lockport before it closed. He stopped at home, dirty but grinning, and asked if I wanted to ride along. On television, Lois Lane was in trouble and Clark Kent had taken off his glasses and had stepped into a phone booth to become Superman. But I could tell by Dad's expectant expression that I must say yes enthusiastically, as if I had always wanted to see what the inside of a bank looked like.

In the car, he told me that he was about to withdraw forty-two hundred dollars so that he could pay Farmer Brown in full for the forty-two acres of land that were blessed by a gushing spring. "That equals a lot of hours at the plant. But I guess I worked and saved hard enough to be doing this. Didn't I?"

"I dunno. I guess so."

In the cavernous bank, his forehead became damp. He shifted his weight from foot to foot and chain smoked as we waited in a long line that flanked a row of faux-marble columns. When he reached the window, he asked the baggy-eyed yawning teller if she had to work much overtime.

"Don't I wish?" she said. "Maybe then I could pay my bills."

She left her window for a few minutes, and I was expecting her to return with a cloth sack bulging with money, the sort that bank robbers were handed on television. But she merely slid my father a single light blue check.

"Thanks." He briefly laughed. "Or I guess so."

Because Harrison Radiator had just spilled a shift of line workers, the traffic was slow outside the bank. But as soon as we crossed into Pendleton, Dad pressed down on the gas peddle, and the rows of telephone poles and mailboxes blurred by on the straight highway that paralleled the canal. He kept reaching into his shirt pocket to be sure that the check was still there, and twice he unfolded it and studied it while driving with one hand on the wheel. By the time we were home, fly ash and coal dust and sweat had ground into the blue paper, staining it darkly like old blood.

After mailing the soiled check to Farmer Brown's lawyer, Dad was frantic to work overtime. "That put quite a hole in our savings," he kept repeating. Even after working a six-day week, he would call the plant on Sunday mornings to see if there was any reason for him to go back.

Yet for a month, the overtime didn't get under his skin and exhaust him as it usually did. He talked so much about his new land and his plans for a cabin and pond that his chatter became background noise, like the humming of the refrigerator. One night he asked, "Do you think we should build the cabin as one room, or divide it into a couple?"

"I scored three touchdowns today," I said. "Nobody could catch me."

Football was my kind of game. While armored hulks beat the crap out of each other, frenzied announcers described tackles as "bone crunching" and long passes as "bombs." Football was nothing like baseball, in which the players were always standing around or grabbing their crotches in a panicky search for something.

I was a rabid fan of the Buffalo Bills, who were the blue-collar defending champs of the upstart American Football League. Many of the players lived all year in western New York and worked during the off-season as ironworkers, truck drivers, or at whatever seasonal work was available. Even a boy could sense that football was the way America worked: a hierarchy of owner and directors and coaches and stars right on down to the grunting anonymous offensive linemen on whose wide shoulder pads every touchdown rested. That summer I received a haircut in a barbershop for the first time, and the barber claimed to be Glenn Bass, a wide receiver for the Bills. I never learned if he really was Bass, but it wouldn't have been unusual then for a professional football player to moonlight as a barber.

One Sunday Dad took me to see the Bills play the Houston Oilers in War Memorial Stadium—or as people in Buffalo referred to that crumbling arena, the Old Rock Pile. He parked the car on the small yellowed front yard of a recently painted house on mostly impoverished and boarded-up Jefferson Avenue and paid the owner a two-dollar fee. We marched to the stadium among a stream of fans watched—predatorily, I imagined—by African Americans sitting on front steps and sagging porches, whole families bemused at the sight of so many whites staring straight ahead with silly terror in their eyes as they hurried through this forgotten neighborhood of the American dream. Ticket scalpers hawked their wares loudly at each intersection, and as the Old Rock Pile came into view Dad whispered for the second time that afternoon, "We'll be lucky if our car isn't stripped when we get back."

Somehow my father, and the rest of us whites worrying toward the stadium, had come to the backward conclusion that African Americans had a history of harming whites. Dad and I had given little thought to what it felt like for the two African Americans who attended my school or the few who worked at the plant, but now we feared being in the minority. Our country had two working classes: one inside and the other out. Inside the thick walls of the stadium, things would be made right again: the coaches and quarterbacks and security guards would be white, like most of the blue-collar fans in the stands.

Our seats were a couple dozen rows above the twenty-yard line—the mythical players of radio and television appearing before me on the great green field as a bright deafening wall of fans rose all around me. With the other forty-five thousand fans, Dad and I cheered and moaned and screamed. As Jack Kemp completed a pass to Goldenwheels Dubenion, I barely noticed that the wildly cheering jumping man in the seat behind me had spilled beer down my back.

After the game, we waited in a long line in the echoing bowels of the stadium to enter the crowded stinking lavatory where the floor was swamped and the loud drunken men pissed into urinals and sinks and corners. Unburdened, we hurried back to the car, and were happier to find it in one piece—believing that to become stranded in the ghetto was certain death—than that the Bills had won.

During the interminable ride out of Buffalo, I almost wished I hadn't gone to the game. Cradling footballs, boys would be spilling outside back in Pendleton, each imagining he was Jack Kemp or Wray Carlton or Goldenwheels Dubenion, and for a while they would play catch and talk about the game, and then would choose up sides while my old man and I were stuck in bumper-to-bumper traffic listening to the same old postgame interviews on the radio.

When the Oilers tied it up, how worried were you?

Well, all I knew was we had to dig deeper in ourself to win it. In the first half, we gave a hundred and ten percent, but we seemed to let up a little and I did start to worry in the second half. But we hung in there and got the job done. It's a big win. Thankfully, Hagood made that interception for us—but you lose as a team and you win as a team. It was a big team win, but from now on we can't relax at all when we get ahead. We need to give a hundred and ten percent the whole game.

The neighborhood game was still underway when I jumped out of the car in our driveway. In the dusk I heard them in the distance on one of the grass lots where we played without helmets or other protective equipment, grunting and cursing and cheering and arguing. I ran into the house to change, then sprinted up the shoulder of the road.

Despite my short legs, I could easily outrun most opposing tacklers. But often I charged straight at the enemy with my head lowered. Sometimes my nose bled, and whenever I found my-self atop a moaning bigger boy, still cradling the football and bleeding and caked with mud, I felt anointed. The television commentator in my mind praised me to millions: "Phillips runs like a tank." Forty-five thousand fans in the stands cheered, stomped, threw plastic beer cups as if confetti. Sitting a couple dozen rows above the twenty-yard line, my father shouted, "That's my boy! That's my boy out there!"

When my father's friend Max came in carrying a six-pack, Dad was at the kitchen table, tracing routes from his new property to surrounding towns. I was back from the neighborhood game, had taken off my muddy sneakers, and was rummaging through the refrigerator. "So whadya think, Jim? They look as bad in that second half as they sounded on the radio or what?"

As Max plunked the moist bottles on the table, Dad looked up as if he had just then noticed his friend. He grinned and said, "Hey, Max."

"So what the hell ya think?"

"They start bulldozing next week."

"Huh?"

"Bulldozing. They start next week."

"What the hell?"

"Bulldozing the pond. I said they start next week."

"You didn't go to the game?"

"Sure I went."

"Then what the hell?" Max grinned and looked over at me and said, "Hey, Mark—-how much your old man have to drink at the Old Rock Pile?"

Dad took three days off work so that he could oversee the building of the pond. By the weekend, when my mother and sisters and I were able to join him on our new land, two roaring bulldozers had finished gouging an oval acre hole in the earth. We spent the freezing night in a canvas tent set up at the edge of the pines, and woke to find an inch of gray water covering an eighth of an acre of clay and rock. Kim and April cheered and threw stones into the big puddle, and I took off my sneakers and socks and sloshed around until my feet were blue and head aching. Dad celebrated by drinking beer before breakfast. Mom began frying eggs and bacon on the portable gasoline stove.

I walked stiffly out of the water on numb feet and asked, "Can we go home pretty soon?"

For the rest of the fall, Dad visited the land alone. Between his overtime at the plant and his time at the new property, I saw little of him until the weekend in late November when my fourteenth birthday was celebrated. My grandparents and some of my aunts and uncles and cousins attended the party, and Mom served a rich homemade chocolate cake. For the first time in my life, none of my birthday presents were toys, games, or balls.

After I modeled my new clothing, Dad carried a dusty high chair up from the cellar and Mom retrieved a pacifier from the attic; everyone laughed as he took a photograph of me squeezed into the chair while sucking on the pacifier and holding the cake with all but one candle removed. After I extracted myself from the chair, Grandfather joked about the timing of my birth: "I still remember it. Jim and me had just stepped out the door and loaded our guns when the guy who lived up the road from the hunting camp we were at showed up to tell us he'd got a call that Markie was being born. It was the first time Markie pissed off his father."

Everyone laughed except Mom. When Dad saw her anger at being reminded that he had been almost one hundred miles away when she had gone into labor, he changed the subject: "Fourteen years old, imagine that. Haven't the years gone fast, Eva?" He looked away before she could reply, and said to his brothers, "When we were fourteen we already had our first jobs."

"Delivering papers," said Uncle Fred.

"Yep," said Dad. "And we didn't keep the money, either."

"Oh no," said Al. "Nope, that went right into Ma's jar."

After supper the next evening, Dad surprised me: "Come with me. I've got another present for you." I followed him into the cellar, where he pointed to a shiny silver and black table saw.

Each evening for a couple of weeks, instead of settling into his easy chair to drink beer and watch the news, he led me into the cellar and tried to teach me to use the table saw and other tools. He was appalled at my ignorance. The first time he asked me to fetch a square, I brought him a level, and he said, "I don't know how you managed to pass wood shop. Who taught it, the home economics teacher?"

Before many weeks had passed, he had built two bird houses, two sets of saw horses, a picnic table, shelves for the

Encyclopedia Britannica that Mom had bought from a door-to-door salesman, and had started to cut lumber for the cabin he planned to raise during the spring. I tried to learn and help, but in part because carpentry bored me and in part because Dad's impatience made me nervous, I couldn't saw straight or hit a nail without bending it over.

Eventually he gave up on me. "Go on up and study," he said. "And you sure better start thinking about going to college, because you sure ain't gonna make a living with your hands." Every so often while I watched the evening news, my father, working alone in the cellar, cutting joists or studs for his cabin, switched on the table saw and exploded a civil rights marcher or antiwar protester into electrostatic.

All that rainy autumn and snowy winter, my father walked through the brick gate house of the power plant past the guard who said good morning to everyone by name. Eight or ten hours later, he again passed the guard who said good-bye as the men took home whatever they wanted. After working overtime one evening, Dad drove his old pickup truck around behind the plant and came out with a twenty-five-foot I-beam for the new cabin and waved at the guard as he drove past the gate house. On another evening he came out with two big rolls of wide rubber conveyor belting to lay on the bottom of the pond near the dock where we would be swimming. And on another with a roll of rubber fire hose so that some of the springwater could be run closer to the cabin.

During lunch break, while the tired men sat on the concrete floor with their backs against the steel lockers, they talked quietly about bowling and the Bills and hunting and fishing and divorces and kids and hippies—and about their dreams. Dad talked about his dream coming true, about his land and cabin. Or he unwrapped his food and ate without speaking, building the cabin in his mind. It would have a tiled concrete floor, sided block walls, a flat tarred roof, and a big stone fireplace. And eventually, when his kids were grown, the cabin would become the bottom floor of a Swiss chalet where he and Mom would retire. Before long, he had built the cabin and chalet so many times in his mind that during his lunch break he could lean back against his locker as if in a lawn chair and close his eyes and feel the sun and breeze on his face while out in the clean cool pond the trout fed and grew and jumped.

He came and went through the brick gate house of the power plant and water rose from the earth and skimmed over the polished stones and slid into the hole. As a December thaw and heavy rain melted the deep snow in the hills, the pond was filled. Water trickled through the overflow, spreading down an open hillside and into a small nameless stream, gurgling through still snowy woods and yellow-green pastures and into manmade Cuba Lake where men jigged for perch and pike through the softening ice.

Eventually the same water, if it could remain the same, splashed over the concrete spillway where the dammed pause was seized anew by the earth and became Oil Creek, engorged by brooks falling from the hills, ribboning and waving through the steep Oil Spring Indian Reservation. And then, suddenly patient, the water wandered through a valley pasture where it eased into brown Olean Creek, widening through the muddy bean fields edging the faintly smoggy town of Olean. Within sight of the bumper-to-bumper traffic on East State Street, some of the groggy drivers still sipping their steaming morning coffee, the water bore into the rising Allegheny River on a path to the Ohio and Mississippi and the sea, swirling past the dikes and factories and streets and power lines, past the finite works of man.

He detected a deepening in the boy's voice and knew what was passing. Kites flown and fish hooked and seats on the twenty-yard line. Encouragement and praise and advice and rules laid down. Scolding and strapping and grounding and the silent treatment and the relief of a hug. A good neighborhood and parents with a good marriage. Hard work and a solid roof and three square meals and a pot to piss in and two nickels to rub together. He wondered what more he could do to help. He saw his meandering son stopping too infrequently to check his bearings—his God and country and father—while stumbling toward manhood.

What a burden, manhood. The very word is heavy on the tongue: men often speak of courage, fortitude, guts, bravery, balls. But rarely of the sacrosanct and transcending and terrifying whole, of manhood. Oh, the imagined weight of it. The father feels it and the boy feels it and they wonder if the boy is beyond succor. What if the boy is doomed to become the wrong kind of man?

Like a young Vietcong, in school I was learning the value of underground resistance: my first lesson came shortly after I'd fought at school. The former police officer who was our principal called us combatants out of our classes, and to me simply said, "This better not happen again." But to the other boy, who had fought in school on other occasions, Mr. Keech said, "You like to fight, huh?" Then he shoved him against a row of lockers again and again until the tough boy was reduced to a sniveler whose snot ran over his lip and down his chin.

No, I didn't plan to become an open rebel and end up as a locker ornament. Instead, when a teacher called on me in class I either said I didn't know the answer or gave an intentionally wrong answer. I rarely did homework or studied, and turned in illegible and incomplete tests. Before long my teachers stopped expecting me to work. And yet they seldom realized I was the one throwing spit wads and making animal noises while they were writing on the blackboard.

One afternoon, I noticed that a teacher's zipper was open. I covered my mouth with my hand and whispered, "Zipper . . . zipper." Several of my classmates were snickering before the teacher realized the cause of their amusement. Rather than simply close the zipper or sit behind his desk, he tried to hide his stained underwear behind the narrow leg of the lectern. More students began whispering, "Zipper . . . zipper. . . zipper" until it was a quiet steady chant. The teacher began to pace rapidly, dragging the lectern around the room in front of him as he stuttered the disjointed lecture. When the snickering became open laughter he strode into the hallway where, facing away from the class, he yanked the zipper upward and caught it on the fabric of his pants. He returned to the room with the zipper partially open and his shirttail rearranged to shield his yellowed underwear. The class roared and several boys doubled over and theatrically fell off their chairs and rolled in the aisles. And yet the blushing teacher resumed stuttering the lecture and dragging the lectern back and forth in front of him until suddenly he threw it on its side.

Screaming threats and ordering two boys to the principal's office, he quieted the class. I was pleased to see that among the doomed was the boy I had fought behind the stairwell.

That spring it became my responsibility to mow our yard and orchard. It was a job, it seemed to me after I had mowed for about ten minutes, that would never end. I especially disliked mowing the orchard, where the ground was bumpy and I had to keep circling trees and picking up branches and stones. I asked Dad how he expected me to study more when he kept giving me work to do around the house.

He pretended he hadn't heard me.

The first time I mowed the orchard, the engine stalled with a banging clatter as I absentmindedly pushed the mower over a stone. Dad rushed out of the house to anxiously inspect the mower, then said, "Who the hell do you think is gonna pay for a new mower when you wreck this one? If you think this job is hard, wait until you see the jobs I'm gonna give you to work off what a new mower will cost me." After I pushed the mower over two more stones, he ordered me to mow with the throttle half closed so it would be less likely that the blade and engine would be damaged. But with less power I had to cut narrower swaths, and it took me four hours instead of two to complete the job.

Gradually, I learned to concentrate on the task. After I hadn't run over any hard objects for two weeks, he allowed me to re-sume mowing with the throttle wide open. Yet I continued to re-sent a job that had to be redone each weekend. I believed he should hire someone to do the mowing. What was the point of working all that overtime, I wondered, if his kid still had to mow the lawn?

By the time that my third dismal report card arrived in the mail, his new land could no longer constantly charm my exhausted father, who for two weeks had been working steady overtime. The land was too far away, the power plant too near. He didn't look at the report card until Sunday afternoon, staring hotly, as if welding the low grades. Then he set about repairing me with a searing lecture about the importance of earning a high school diploma. Later that evening Mom asked if something was troubling me. I said no, while thinking, Of course! You, my teachers, stupid schoolwork, the cheap clothes you buy me! Everything!

Mom found me a tutor and Dad grounded me until the school year was over. But long before my final report card of the year arrived, my parents, teachers, and tutor had given up on me. My parents went along with a guidance counselor's suggestion that I repeat even the subjects that I had somehow passed, English and history. By then I had conned even myself into believing I was dim-witted.

A few evenings into summer vacation, I was in my backyard with Johnny Burbidge and David Nasca when Kim leaned out her bedroom window and lilted, "Mark failed ninth grade, Mark failed ninth grade, Mark failed ninth grade."

"You did?" asked David, who was the top student in his grade.

I ran into the house, charged up the stairs, and punched Kim on the shoulder. She howled for Dad, who looped justice double before coming after me. He swung the belt at my back and legs and ass and I stood and took it without crying out. Kim pled, "Daddy! Please stop!"

Suddenly he did stop. And without saying anything, he turned and walked away.

I never hit my sister again.

My father hit me only once more.

Following the strapping, he gave me the silent treatment for two days. I gave it to him for longer. During the third day of my acting as if he didn't exist, he asked if I planned to stay mad at him forever. Without replying, I walked out of the living room where we had been watching television. He caught up with me in the kitchen, wrapped one arm around my neck, and tickled my ribs with his free hand until I couldn't help but laugh. My laughter enraged me. I broke free, spun around, and punched his stomach. For a brief moment we stood looking into into each other's eyes with surprise and fear, and then suddenly he pushed me onto my back, sat on my chest, and punched my nose just hard enough to bloody it.

After dinner the next day, he asked me if I wanted to go fishing in the canal.

While watching ducks and muskrats swim by our red and white bobbers, we talked a little about the fish we weren't catching. When it was almost dark, we talked about my intention to study harder during my second year in the ninth grade.

We bounced up Route 16, a two-lane road that snakes out of Buffalo, sneaks through suburbs, and rises into the Alleghenies. The sun still rested orange on the treetops, but already the day was sweltering. On the seat between Dad and me, Heidi panted and shed clumps of fur, and I kept pushing her away and saying "yep" as if sincerely listening to Dad's chatter. Whenever one of the front wheels of his old pickup crashed into a deep pothole, my head banged against the cab roof. I silently wondered why he didn't buy one of those new trucks with heavy-duty shock absorbers Ford had been advertising on television.

He pointed out the patient heron waiting hunch-shouldered for a trout to slip into the shimmering riffles of Ischua Creek, the laboriously flapping hawk dangling a writhing snake, the velvety whitetail buck in the plush meadow. But I wasn't interested. I was too full of my own nature. I wanted to be back home with my friends and considered myself a hostage. I thought about girls, and I shifted my hands over my lap to hide the bulge. I felt pimples sprouting and ached to pop them. I had more important things to do than help build a cabin in the middle of nowhere. After a while I closed my eyes and felt only the queasiness of travel sickness. I was relieved that I'd remembered to bring along my transistor radio. Without it, there would be nothing to do at night except watch the campfire.

Dad turned off Route 16 in downtown Ischua: a tiny corner store, a white church, a volunteer fire department, a small cluster of cavernous old homes. We bounced over the potholes of School Street and then onto a narrow back road rising into the hills, where in most places the terrain was too rocky and precipitous for even hardscrabble dairy farming. The forest edged up to the hunting camps and house trailers set on the occasional plots of gentle land squeezed between the hillsides and road. Eventually he turned onto a dirt road that cut through abandoned farmland. The truck, throwing up a billowing wake of dust, rattled to the bottom of a steep hill. There he turned onto a new gravel driveway that ran eight hundred feet to his dream.

Even there I didn't understand his longing to possess the reaching white pines, the overflowing pond so clear we could see the hardpan beneath nine feet of water, the little cabin he planned to build. I thought about my friends back home having fun. Then I saw the depressingly large pile of sand and gravel that we would use to make concrete after we had finished digging the foundation trenches for the cabin. And behind us I heard Grandfather's pickup crunching up the driveway.

I helped unload the bags of food, cement mixer, gasoline generator, lumber, and other tools and supplies. Dad ordered me to place the perishables and some of the beer and pop in the spring, and then to set up the tent. After I completed those tasks I thought I deserved a rest, but Dad was already digging the cabin foundation where he had driven stakes and strung line the previous weekend. He tossed a pick and shovel my way. Grandfather was busy constructing an outhouse. I felt as if I were in a movie in which wilderness homesteaders raced to build a cabin as winter approached. But Dad and Grandfather were on vacation from their jobs and were preparing to build a mere hunting cabin. I wondered what it was that caused adults to hurry so.

At first the thick wooden pick handle felt heavy and unbalanced in my hands, but before long I was swinging it smoothly. The topsoil was dark and soft, easily loosened with the wide blade of the pick and thrown aside with a shovel. But below the topsoil we struck dense gray clay laced with stone; the pick easily crumbled sandstone but merely threw sparks when striking pieces of shale. And the deeper we dug the harder the ground became. A foot above the frost line, we hit layers of shale fused by thin layers of clay and iron. We had to switch to the pointed blades of the picks and grunted as we swung, our bodies jolted each time we drove the tempered steel another half an inch into the earth to pry loose a little more rock.

When Grandfather walked over, Dad and I had been working on the first length of trench for three hours. He laughed and said, "Looks like you guys been fucking the dog."

Smiling and shaking his head, Dad climbed out of the trench and wiped his brow. "I never thought ground could be so hard. How's your end going, George?"

"Done, Jim."

"All done?"

"You don't see the dog following me around, do you?"

As Grandfather gave us the grand tour of the outhouse, he said, "This beats an indoor toilet any day. Don't you think so, Markie?"

He wasn't kidding: on his farm he used the outhouse except in the coldest weather. Once I had asked him why, and he had laughed and said, "You don't shit in your *house,* do you, Markie?"

Straddling a square pit, the outhouse was constructed of rough-cut lumber. It had two seats, ample leg and head room, and a small glass window that could be slid open. Attached to a wall was a wooden placard with the message *If we all is paper hogs we'll have ta go back to catalogs,* and on another wall was a calendar with an illustration of a deer hunter shitting in the woods as a big buck pranced by. Grandfather had already equipped the outhouse with a roll of toilet paper and a coffee can filled with lye. And as he ran one of his dirty and calloused hands over the rough cover of the larger seat, I could tell he was looking forward to his next bowel movement. I wouldn't have been surprised if he had brought along a jar of prune juice.

When the tour was finished, Grandfather gulped water from a gallon milk jug, stripped off his shirt, grabbed a pick, and climbed into the trench that Dad and I had been digging. Grandfather was a few years shy of sixty, bald, toothless, and his potbelly was blanketed with dense gray hair. But his arms and shoulders were hard and his back and neck rippled with muscle as he swung the pick; in a blur of wood and metal and sparks and flying stone, he dug without speaking. Dad and I labored faster than we had been doing, but Grandfather was loosening more shale than the two of us combined and kept up that pace for the remainder of the afternoon.

When we had dug two of the four trenches, we stopped for the day. In the pond, I bathed naked, the cool water soothing my blistered hands, cleansing me of sweat and clay. I swam on my back, gazing into the clear sky as the sun dipped, and didn't leave the water until my teeth were chattering and lips blue.

The men had built a fire in a circle of rocks. Wrapped in a towel, I warmed myself with my back to the flames until one of the rocks exploded, scattering shards over the pond and sending me running minus the towel, to Grandfather's great amusement. When only embers remained of the fire, Dad sent me to fetch the burger, beer, and pop from the spring and a grill from the truck. Soon the bluish smoke of burning fat drippings was drifting low over the pond where feeding swallows were circling and dipping for mayflies. As the men drank from wet brown bottles, I asked Dad why he drank his beer cold only at the cabin. "The spring," he replied.

After we ate, darkness stole and Grandfather added more wood to the fire. The men finished their beer and were quiet. I watched the flames and never thought about turning on my transistor radio. Eventually the men said good night and slid into their sleeping bags. I sat up a little longer before confining Heidi to the pickup. Then because I knew the tent would be full of beer farts, I spread my sleeping bag several feet away, on pine needles, beneath boughs that hung almost to the ground. Within minutes I fell asleep to the sound of sap dripping on the sleeping bag.

At dawn, I woke to Grandfather's singing in the outhouse. When I sat up I discovered that my back and arms were stiff and sore and that my blistered hands burned. As I shuffled toward Dad, who was boiling water and frying breakfast on the portable gasoline stove, I considered faking illness. But listening to Grandfather's singing, I became ashamed of myself. I said good morning and sat down on a lawn chair and merely moaned a little to let Dad know I was sore. I drank a cup of hot chocolate, snuck behind the outhouse, shook a bush, and deepened my voice into a long growl. "Hey!" Grandfather shouted. "What's my wife doing here?"

By that evening, we had finished digging the trenches. The next morning, Grandfather left for home to catch up on his farm work, and Dad proposed we take the day off. After breakfast, in the brook below the pond I caught darting creek chubs and backward-spurting crawfish in a tin can. Then I built a dam of rock, sticks, and sod. Next I followed the water downstream into a brushy woods of young maple and poplar. When I returned from the hike, I began enlarging the dam, and by the time that Dad called to me, fearing I'd become lost, I had backed up a sizable pool of water. I looked up and was startled at how far the sun had traveled since morning.

Early the next morning we started filling the trenches with concrete. Into the turning mixer Dad shoveled five parts of gravel and sand to each part of cement, and I carried pails of water from the pond, pouring slowly into the mixer until he determined that the churning and rolling soup was the proper consistency. The old gasoline generator labored, the motor spitting streams of oily smoke. When the first batch was ready, Dad swung the steel lever, pouring the cement into the large wheelbarrow I was steadying. "You think you can handle that?"

"I'll be okay."

I strained to lift the wooden handles and momentarily feared I couldn't move the load, but then the rubber tire began to crunch gravel. I was barely able to bring the weight to a stop again, my heels digging in as I was dragged toward the trench. Then I squatted and straightened, lifting and pouring the load, and was disheartened by how insignificant the splattered concrete appeared at the bottom of the trench. Still, after several loads I stopped counting and barely looked into the trench anymore. I fell into the rhythm of manual labor, and the noise of the mixer and generator became a kind of mechanical music, and I carried and poured water and pushed the wheelbarrow and dumped the loads with little variation or thought.

By evening the trenches were almost half-full. Before crawling into the tent for the night, we put the dog in the cab of the truck and covered the mixer, generator, and bags of cement with sheets of plastic. Later that night the sagging sky burst, the sides of the tent flapping in the saturated wind.

When we woke in the morning, the canvas was leaking. Wearing ponchos, we hid the mixer and lumber in the pines, and loaded the rest of our supplies and gear onto the truck. Dad said, "Well, Mark, considering how hard the ground was, we did pretty good. Don't you think?"

"Yep."

He added that he would have waited out the rain except for his back pain, which had kept him awake much of the night. I expressed surprise that he had back trouble, and he said, "This is the first I knew it, too."

He believed that the persisting pain was caused by a hard bump his lower back had taken from the corner of a boiler door. His doctor agreed.

On Saturday evening, I asked if I could go to a party. Normally Dad would have grilled me and I would have claimed there would be no alcohol and that we teens would be strictly supervised by adults, and eventually he might have said, "Sure, Mark, go ahead if you want." Then after a moment he would have added, "I think maybe I'll stop in later. Maybe your friend's parents could use some help." And I would have stayed home. But this time he was in bed with a heating pad under his lower back and had just washed down three aspirin with a shot of whiskey. As Mom took away the shot glass, he simply said, "Go ahead."

In a clattering and backfiring Chevrolet with gaping rust holes and no front bumper, an older boy gave me a ride to the party.

For a steep fee, he also presented me with a pint of whiskey, a smooth amber bottle of illicit confidence. At the cramped house where our host lived with her mother and younger sister, I shuffled in through a kitchen of wisecracking teens. As the line moved down a short hallway, I passed the living room where the girl's mother was gazing at the television, fingering an icy mixed drink. The sound of the television couldn't be heard over the rock music vibrating the floor, and as the line slowly descended the cellar stairs, the noise assaulted me.

From the bottom of the stairs I could see only a shadowy jumble of bodies faintly illuminated by the orange glow of cigarettes and the dull blue light of the phonograph console. The stream of youths behind me pushed me farther into the crowd. Boys and girls were laughing and slapping me on the back, lips moving in a dim haze of smoke, yelling words muffled by the music. We communicated with back slaps, waves, raised middle fingers. Everywhere bottles and cups tipped up and down and up and down, as if bobbing on a sea. Eventually, the back door was opened, releasing the unbearable heat and spilling kids outside.

In the backyard I took a big gulp of my whiskey, eyes watering. But just as I began to feel relaxed and welcome, a hulking drunken junior demanded that I share my booze. I ran around the house and into the front yard, where I dove into the thick shrubbery. Concealed by branches and leaves, I began to feel sorry for myself: rumors had been spreading about so-and-so and so-and-so fucking in a bedroom or car or under the cellar stairs, but I was alone, hiding from a Neanderthal who desired the whiskey that had cost me a month of my allowance. I unscrewed the cap, pinched my nose, and downed half the pint.

Then I spit into the remaining whiskey, crawled out of my hiding spot, located my stalker, and tossed him the bottle.

The burning in my throat and stomach soon became inane joy spreading to the tips of my fingers and toes. I became a rock star singing into a paper cup and a loud jaunty comedian and a hot lover pinching the asses of girls. And eventually, on my hands and knees in the cellar, I puked on a shoe that someone had shed. The last thing I recalled before rolling over and blacking out was a fuzzy and spinning boy pointing down at me and laughing silently.

David Nasca located and woke me after the police had arrived for the second time. He helped me to my feet, led me outside, encouraged me to puke again, and steadied me while we walked the three miles to his home. He gave me coffee and Alka-Seltzer, washed and dried my clothing, and made me laugh by describing the look that had come over a girl's face when, in the dim cellar, she had slipped her bare foot back into her shoe.

When I woke on Sunday morning, I was happy because on Monday at school I would be a topic of conversation: "Man, did you see how plastered Phillips got?" But as I pulled on a pair of blue jeans, my bladder aching, I became dizzy and nauseated.

Balancing myself by pressing my right palm against the wall, I slowly descended the stairs and crossed the kitchen where my parents were eating breakfast. I asked Dad how his back was feeling, and he said it felt much better. The odor of fried bacon intensified the nausea and I hurried down the hallway to the bathroom. While I pissed, I gulped antacid. Then I sat on the edge of the bathtub, my head resting in my hands, until Mom knocked on the door and asked, "Are you okay in there?"

"Yes," I said, standing up too quickly. "Just a second." I waited for my equilibrium to return before I opened the door.

They were standing in the hallway. Dad said, "You look sick."

"Yeah, I got an upset stomach."

"Well, you better eat some breakfast anyhow. We've got a lot of work to do around here today."

"I'm sick, Dad."

"Of course you are. One look tells me that. What did you put in your stomach last night?"

I hung my head.

"Of course you're sick. And if you do that when you're a man, you'll have to get up early the next morning and go to work. So you better get used to it."

I declined breakfast, but all morning I helped Dad clean the garage and cellar. I was quiet, but his back pain had gone away for the time being and he talked a great deal, especially about his new property in the hills. He made no further mention of my nausea or its cause, even after I ran out of the cellar to vomit antacid on the back lawn.

By midafternoon, my stomach had settled and I was hungry. Dad was roasting hot dogs on a portable charcoal grill in the front yard. In the shade of the maples, Mom spread two blankets on the lawn. Kim and April carried out the silverware and paper plates and the rest of the food.

Dad and I in our dirty work clothes and Mom and the girls still in their church dresses, we sat on the blankets and ate. Mowers growled throughout the neighborhood. April chattered between each bite as Dad repeatedly wiped ketchup from the end of her roll before it could drip on her dress. Whispering and giggling, Mom and Kim were watching Mr. Westfall wash his car in the driveway across the street.

I finished eating in silence, cleaned my hands on a napkin, and stretched out on a blanket softly lumped by clumps of grass. I gazed up through an opening in the maple canopy, the view changing from blue to white to blue again. Then I closed my eyes. I was almost asleep when Dad said, "Mark, the lawn needs mowing today. But I guess it can wait until tomorrow."

I kept my promise and improved my grades, even though I would soon forget the scientific names of the earth's layers, the capital of Morocco, why the Seven Years War was fought, and how to solve an algebraic equation. But I well recall the girl who sat next to me in algebra class, her long legs crossed and right foot swinging, nylons grinding, black miniskirt inching up her beautiful thighs. I recall how ancient my teachers seemed and that I preferred counting floor tiles to listening to their lectures. I recall the windows open on hot days and the beckoning odor of mowed grass. And yet somehow, during my second year in the ninth grade, I learned to suppress my classroom longings for the girl, my desire to run free on the grass, my contempt for the teachers.

What I couldn't suppress was a strange urge to repeatedly draw, in my notebooks, a cabin that was supported by a thick wooden platform extending from the side of a stone cliff. But I found that if I drew the cabin at the start and end of each class, I could pay attention to the teacher in between. I also found that the trick to taking good notes was to turn note taking into an obsession, like drawing the cabin. My hand and wrist aching, I filled page after page with information that I would forget soon after I had passed the tests. It was natural to long for open spaces and leggy girls, but I had become disciplined. My shrugs, grunts, and most of my other old tics had been replaced by masked tics or obsessions, such as drawing the precarious cabin, repeatedly changing my breathing pattern, curling my toes within the privacy of my sneakers, taking detailed notes of dry facts, and repeatedly raising my hand to ask my teachers for clarifications. Only one of my old tics was still a persistent problem in school. My eyes still blinked mercurially, like those of a nervous impostor. I became known as Blinky Phillips.

My parents worried about me. Almost every evening they asked about school and remained skeptical even when I showed them tests I'd passed. Dad worried about me while for the ten thousandth time he walked through the gate house of the power plant, or tasted the bitter coal dust that had soiled the pain pills a doctor had prescribed for his sore back. Mom worried while washing Dad's work clothes that were full of burn holes, or scrubbing door hinges with an old toothbrush, or cleaning the thin cracks between floor tiles with a needle. They wondered if their son had enough self-discipline to graduate from high school.

One evening, when my upstairs bedroom was sultry and I was doing my English homework at the kitchen table, Dad sat down opposite me. "I hope you keep this up," he said. "Just remember that if you don't graduate from school, the best job you can hope for is someplace like Harrison Radiator. Lifting radiator cores from one line to another all day or something. But I don't even know about that. You don't have to be a hard worker to do a job like that, just dull enough or doped enough. And you're not stupid." Gripping a bottle of warm beer, he walked into the living room. From the kitchen I could see Mom, who had been washing the picture window, pause to study the coffee table as the television blared a jingle for furniture polish.

I finished diagraming sentences. Before studying for a multiple choice test in geography, I tore a sheet of paper from my looseleaf binder and drew the precarious cabin.

———⟫◆⟪———

As he reaches into the tangled pile of brush for the spirits, Horace Guild says, "You durst not tell Mother about this." He removes the cork with his teeth. He threads his thickly calloused index and middle fingers through and around the small oval handle and swings up the gallon jug, the bottom supported by his forearm and the side resting on his shoulder as he drinks so deeply that the two boys gasp. Then he says, "Your turn."

They look at him as if he has lost his mind.

He laughs. "Fifteen years of it and now we're done. Seventy acres cleared of wilderness and you helped. You more than helped. You helped like men. And now you deserve a drink."

After a moment, the youngest says, "No thank you, Papa."

They won't look at him.

"We just drunk from the spring," says the oldest.

"That was cold. This is hot."

"No thank you."

"She won't smell it," he says, and pulls from a pocket three withered leeks. "Not only are these good for getting you sent home from school."

"Mother will have supper. Can we go?"

"Yes . . . go." As they turn away, he adds, more softly, "You are good boys." And as they cross the spring carrying the crosscut saw between them, he asks, "You won't breathe a word of this?"

After a few more long steps, and without looking back, the oldest replies faintly, "We shan't."

"I'll be to supper."

With the gliding strides of boys who are almost men, Willis and Charles slide past the abandoned cabin and the gaunt feeding cattle in the pasture dotted with dark stumps, and then for a few minutes he can't see them as they cross the trickling stream in the gully, and then they come up out of the gully and into the green field of winter wheat, their strides shortening as they climb the hill. Now they have their faces turned to each other and are gesturing with their free hands as they talk about their father. Sitting on a small hump of land above the spring, he watches them reach the frame house at the road atop the hill and drop the saw and run through the doorway, no doubt telling her already. He grins and takes another swig from the ceramic jug before replacing the cork.

All of his land has been cleared except for a thirty-acre plot of maple and beech saved for sugar bush and firewood. New neighbors, also clearing land at a furious rate, have become as thick as flies on a horse's rump. The elk and cougar are gone now and the wolf almost, and in the remaining forest a man is more likely to see browsing cattle or rooting pigs than a deer or bear. Horace needs to finish digging and pulling up the stumps and roots of the virgin trees, and after that, he sees, there will be only farming and more farming until he dies.

How long has he dreamt of this moment, the land cleared? In his dream house, on the parlor wall, he has hung in a frame the crude map that guided David Hibner and him through the wilderness. And yet when he looks at that yellowed and torn map from now on, he will want to follow it in the opposite direction, so they can start out all over again.

Up on the porch of the house they are ringing the bell, time for supper, time, time, time. Between the clangs he can hear the murmuring and swallowing of the icy spring.

Finitude

Most of our adult relatives and neighbors knew that my father had prostate cancer. And some also knew that to slow the spread of the cancer, which was fueled by testosterone and had already reached inoperable locations in his back and hips, the surgeons would remove his healthy testicles along with his prostate gland. But my sisters and I didn't know. One evening at supper, he said, "You know that back pain I've been having? Well, I've got what they call a slipped disc. And next week I gotta go into the hospital to get operated on."

I commented that the operation sounded dangerous, but he assured us it was routine. "Believe me," he added, "I'm lucky that's all that's wrong with me."

He wanted Mom to spend as much time as she could with him at the hospital, but worried that my sister Kim and I, although thirteen and fifteen years old, weren't responsible enough to take good care of April. And so two days before the surgery he asked Grandmother to stay at our house while he was hospitalized. But she complained that she was behind in her housework, and he mumbled, "Oh, okay," and hung up the receiver without saying good-bye. He sat down at the kitchen table.

Mom asked, "What did she say?"

"Your mother said no."

"She said no?"

"She said no."

"But why?"

He didn't answer. After a few moments he stood and moved back around the counter to where the telephone was mounted on the kitchen wall. He dialed his brother Al's house and asked Aunt Doris if she would stay with us.

Toting a suitcase and a shoe box full of recipes, Aunt Doris arrived with a big smile and soon had chattered thousands of words without coming up for air. But by the fifth day of her stay, all that could be heard from her was grunting as she bent over to pick up clothing, shoes, sneakers, phonograph records, toys, and school books. On the sixth morning, she telephoned Al to complain about us. He told her it was time that Kim and I learned to take care of April, not to mention ourselves. Doris had her suitcase and shoe box packed when my sisters and I arrived home from school, and told us what she thought, beginning with, "No wonder your grandmother didn't want to come here." When Mom returned from the hospital that night and learned why Doris had gone, she said, "No wonder my mother didn't want to stay here."

The next afternoon, Mom came home to cook and eat supper, left April with a neighbor, then returned to the hospital with Kim and me. I expected Dad to be angry that Kim and I had taken advantage of Doris. He was. But it was my hair, covering the tops of my ears, that he mentioned as soon as I walked into the room.

Even though he had given me permission to grow it out long enough to comb, he demanded to know if I liked looking like a girl and if I was a homosexual. He asked Mom why she hadn't brought the electric hair clipper along. He ordered me to squat next to the hospital bed so that he could examine my scalp, and claimed it was dirty and full of sores. Suddenly he shouted, "Is that my doctor I hear coming up the hall? Jesus Christ, I don't want him seeing any son of mine looking like a girl."

After a few more days in the hospital, Dad was released. The first thing he did after he entered our home was to hug each of us children. Then he limped into his and Mom's bedroom and shut the door. Except to use the bathroom, he didn't come out for two days.

Although it was but a pause between a high and low tide in his life, on the second afternoon of his seclusion something happened that let Dad feel he could swim in any direction he wanted.

Mom was grocery shopping and my sisters and I were at school. From his bed, he heard knocking on the front door. Then he heard the door open. Someone called, "Hello?" The door closed and the kitchen floor creaked as someone walked slowly across it asking, "Is anyone home? Hello? Anybody here?"

Dad reached beneath the bed for the pistol and ammunition he had been keeping there since his return from the hospital. But they were gone. Now the footsteps and voice were in the hallway outside his bedroom, and he didn't know if he was angrier at the intruder or at Mom for having removed the weapon he had been intending to use if he decided to kill himself.

The bedroom door banged open and my unshaven, red-eyed father charged out in wrinkled pajamas, fists clenched: "Just what the hell do you think you're up to, buddy?"

The thin balding man in the hallway, backpedaling so hurriedly that he stumbled, stuttered that he was our family's minister and was paying a visit to the sick. He said he would return at a more convenient time.

When my sisters and I came home from school, Dad was dressed and shaven and was repairing a drippy faucet in the kitchen. April dropped her lunch pail and ran to him with open arms. I asked how his back was feeling. Stooping with a grimace to hug April, he replied that he felt so good that in the morning he might return to work.

At supper, he told our family about the intruder. He claimed that because he attended church no more than once or twice each year, he hadn't recognized the minister. But Dad had a good memory, and I suspected that he not only had recognized the minister, but had recognized his distinctive voice before seeing his face. I could see that Mom was embarrassed by the incident, but I didn't like the minister and was glad.

All seemed well again in our home. Our father had frightened away God's messenger.

David Nasca was on the phone, breathlessly announcing that his older sister and three of her friends were swimming in his family's little above-ground pool. And one of her friends was "blonde, built like Brigitte Bardot, and has on the fucking stringiest bikini you've ever seen."

I arrived poolside just after Johnny Burbidge, holding in his stomach, dove into the water and came up ogling. David was floating in an inner tube, ogling. Ogling, I prepared to dive from the deck. But David's sister looked up and asked, "Holy shit, how many of you little perverts do you think can fit in this pool?"

I stepped out of the way as she climbed out, followed by her indignant friends. As the girls marched to the house, water must have streamed from their matted hair and down their bronzed backs, and blades of mowed grass must have stuck to their angular feet. But we boys saw only the round and firm derriere of young Bardot, swinging gracefully away from our clumsy lust. We swam for a few more minutes, our genitals shrinking, before we, too, left the pool.

Barefoot on David's blacktopped driveway, hoping that the girls were watching from the house, we played basketball. We took long arching jump and hook shots, affecting grace, while swapping lies about our sex lives. The lies grew and the shots came harder, the backboard shaking and hoop rattling, and we began stripping the ball, blocking shots, driving for layups. After pulling a rebound away from Johnny, David backed onto the lawn for a long shot and tried changing the subject from sex to the New York Yankees. But Johnny and I, fighting for position beneath the backboard, were not yet in the mood for a new subject. And soon the lies became epics. After claiming that I'd had sex in the cellar of my church, I leapt for a rebound and was knocked to the blacktop by Johnny.

Eventually it was I who saved us, accidentally, from each other. Suddenly thinking how unlikely it was that I would ever experience more than fabricated sex, I said, "My old man says I gotta get an even shorter haircut for the summer." Usually my complaints about Dad elicited sympathy from my friends, but this time it was as if I'd announced that I'd taken out a contract on his life. As the basketball bounced up the driveway and rolled into the open garage, they said that Dad was right to make me get a haircut. When I saw they weren't kidding, I pointed out that their hair was much longer than mine. They claimed they planned to get haircuts soon. "It's too hot to have long hair in the summer," said David.

"Yeah," added Johnny, "and this is the time of year when you can get lice and stuff."

Then Johnny turned his back to me and whispered something to David, who shook his head no. For a few seconds neither of them would look at me. Then David patted my back and said, "We complain about our parents too much. It wouldn't hurt us to try and make them happy once in a while. Would it?"

I studied his face, convinced it must be true that jerking off causes insanity. Finally I shrugged and replied, "I dunno. I guess maybe not."

We stood in the driveway, halfheartedly rehashing our plans for the summer, before saying good-bye. On the front lawn, David's old dog Ginger was sleeping in the shade of a small maple. With windows open, cars and pickup trucks were speeding up and down the road: our fathers were on their way home from work.

Three days later, my father sat waiting for something, smiling slightly, looking across the table at Kim and me. Mom wound a dish towel around her left wrist, pulled it tight, unwound it. Finally he said, "I got some bad news. We still don't want April to know—that's why she's not home. She's still pretty young."

He paused and shrugged before continuing, still faintly smiling. "We didn't want to tell you, either—or not yet anyhow. But one of the kids in the neighborhood heard his parents talking about it, and so we want you to hear it from us before you hear it from someone else."

I had no reason to believe that my parents were having marital trouble, but all I could think of was that they were getting a divorce.

Then he took a deep breath, lowered his eyes, and told us he had cancer that had started in "a gland called the prostate." He explained that the cause of his back pain had been misdiagnosed for nearly a year because it was very unusual for a man who was only forty to develop prostate cancer. He added that the surgeons had not operated on his back: they had removed his prostate. But the cancer had spread into his bones, where it couldn't be removed, and was of a type that couldn't be treated. The doctors weren't sure how long he would live: maybe a year, maybe five.

He didn't mention the castration.

Kim's eyes filled with tears, and she jumped up to hug him. I walked out of the house. In the backyard, staring out over the weeds and brush of abandoned farmland, I was terrified. Death was something that happened on phony television shows, to grandparents, and to the careless boy in my grade who was hit by a car. But fathers didn't die. You depended on them for your food and clothing, to whup your ass when you needed it, and to repair things that broke. After a teacher yanked my ear so hard that it turned black and blue, Dad had charged into the school to seize the teacher by the tie and let him know whose kid he had messed with. But cancer could kill both of my fathers, the threatening and the protecting, the one who had been working too much and the one who hadn't. It would be the ultimate silent treatment. Who would head my family? Would I still have a family? I looked around wildly, half expecting a black cloud to spew a tornado. But the sky was blue and the air still; a cicada was rasping. I hurried back inside.

That night in bed I thought about what Dad had said. To me five years was a very long time; in five years maybe they would find a cure for cancer. I fell asleep remembering our family vacation when he dove into Chautauqua Lake, leaving me alone in a motorboat. He had finally surfaced on the opposite side of the boat, my fear popping like a bubble, my father alive and grinning and waving a small white stone, the wet surface glittering like a miracle in the sunlight.

He was in a hurry to finish building the cabin while he could. On weekends, he and I poured the floor and sided the block walls with paneling. Whenever his pain became severe, I put away the tools and machinery and stayed with him until he fell asleep on a cot, drugged with Darvon, the radio turned low—Mary Hopkin singing "Those Were the Days" in a year when Martin Luther King, Jr. and Bobby Kennedy had been assassinated.

While he dozed, I sometimes trained for the junior varsity football season by jogging on the steep dirt roads of Ischua. But more often, I fished in the pond, dammed brooks with sticks and sod and stones, or stretched out in meadows to daydream with sunshine on my face. Football season was still several weeks away, and I had almost forever in which to do whatever I wanted.

Dad took his second week of vacation in November to go deer hunting. Various buddies had let him know they needed a place to hunt, but as if observing them in a dream of which they were unaware, he now felt somewhat distant from his healthy friends. Anyhow, he disliked the usual deer camp where men stayed up all night gambling and drinking; he intended to hunt alone. Mom worried, but he promised her he would stay close to the cabin.

She packaged several prepared meals, which he placed in the spring to prevent spoilage or freezing. When he returned to the cabin in the evenings he lit the propane lights and built a wood fire in the heatilator of the unfinished fireplace. After eating a supper warmed on the propane stove, he slid beneath the heavy blankets of the lower bunk and watched the wavering light of the popping and crackling fire reflecting off the ceiling and walls until Darvon closed his eyes.

He hunted close to the cabin, but trespassed on the land of the Twin Ridge Conservation Club, where from the crotch of a tree he watched for deer and members of the hunting club. On his third morning in the tree, he killed a small buck, then dragged it two hundred yards before gutting it on the edge of his own land. He concealed the incriminating trail by brushing the snow with pine boughs. Then he popped Darvon and gulped whiskey and stayed in bed until the pain subsided in the evening.

Mom woke my sisters and me when Dad arrived home with the hollow and red-bellied buck in the back of the pickup, its eyes open and glassy and its stiff tongue jutting from its mouth. In our pajamas and slippers we ran across the white powdery lawn to where the truck was parked in the driveway, our proud father trailing us, and climbed up to touch the coarse cold fur.

After the meal Horace slips away, as he has on every Independence Day since the war, from his children and grandchildren gathered on the farm for the annual family picnic, down the wheat field with his head hanging, stiffly over a split rail fence, carefully over the narrow stony creek bed, and with slow difficulty up the weedy pasture to where a clump of transplanted beech and maple and ash shade the spring. He can feel his family watching him and imagines what is said with irritated laughter: "It's the pioneer in him. When his elbows begin to rub, he heads out."

"Pioneer, nothing," says his son William. "He's got a jug of spirits stashed down there."

But it is because whenever he sees his surviving children and grandchildren together on Independence Day, his sorrow sprouts for his two dead sons, as if watered by the easy joy of the young. Near the spring he sits on the hillside beneath an ash and tries to forget about Willis shot at Chancellorsville during the hopeless charge. How long was his body picked at by crows and smothered by flies in the sun until dragged into a shallow grave by a stranger? And before his days of delirium in Andersonville Prison, did Charles ask one of the five other captured Union soldiers from Ischua to give a message to his family? Horace will never know, because like Charles all five were starved to death.

He comes to the spring to put the war out of his mind. He comes to remember something else, like pouring fresh water into a cup to displace the stale. He recalls when Willis and Charles were still young boys, when after a prayer meeting on the Burlingame farm they asked him to take them fishing. By then only dace could survive in the exposed warmed stream below the house, so they hiked to Farwell Gulch and down it until the ravine was too narrow and steep for logging and they could see, in the shade of the big

hemlocks and pines, countless small finning trout in the clear current waiting for a mayfly or nymph to float or tumble downstream.

He and Willis caught several easily, but Charles insisted on fishing
farther downstream in a deeper pool and hooked nothing until a large brook
trout swallowed the worm and hook and Charles screamed for help as it
splashed and dove. By the time Horace arrived, the fish had tangled the line
on a submerged tree limb, but he could faintly see its form among the
branches, still fighting the line. He yanked off his boots and britches and
waded into the water. And though the cold took his breath away, he squatted and followed the line with his hand until he felt the smooth fish and
slipped a finger into a gill and lifted out the splendrous wiggling trout.

The boys cheered, then began to guffaw, and at first Horace didn't
realize they were laughing at the sight of him without his britches in the
freezing water.

To better remember, he slips his right hand into the spring.

Tenses

I had to pee so bad that I wanted to charge over the kid in front of me and sprint to the urinal. But I was embarrassed to ask the track coach if I could leave practice to go wee wee, and so I kept panting and crunching around and around in the sun on the hot black cinders. With every aching stride I wondered how long I could go without pissing down my legs.

Quite a while, it turned out. And after practice the coach was impressed to see me run from the track to the locker room while my exhausted teammates walked. I charged right up to the urinal. While gasping for air and reading something obscene scrawled in ink on the tiled wall, I felt burning as I began to empty my hurting bladder. I looked down and saw the startling red. A few seconds passed before I understood that my urine was full of blood.

Mom took me to a pediatrician, who concluded that I had merely strained my bladder. But Dad told his urologist about me, and the urologist wasn't so inclined to dismiss my bleeding. Because Dad had developed prostate cancer at such an early age, the urologist feared that my family genes were fatal or that the lot of us had been exposed to a potent carcinogen.

165

The urologist put me in the hospital for two days. He squeezed my prostate until I yelped, ordered blood and urine tests, had various organs x-rayed, and threaded a tiny camera up my urethra while I was under general anesthetic.

Then he discharged me and said he would call with the results.

During the ride home from the hospital, I drummed my thighs with my palms and hummed a tune. Dad asked, "Aren't you worried?"

It hadn't occurred to me that I actually had anything to worry about. Adults were always giving you pills or shots or were nagging you to brush your teeth and eat right. Adults worried a lot. I was a member of the track team and a junior varsity football star pursued by junior varsity cheerleaders. I shrugged. "Not really."

"That's good, I guess. It's good not to worry too much."

I was bouncing a rubber ball off the back of the garage when the doctor called and gave the good news to my father. And when I looked up and saw Dad on the back lawn walking toward me, he was grinning and crying.

On a morning soft with cherry blossoms, the curtains fluttered as he sat up and stretched. His face was puffy and eyes slitted, but he climbed out of bed spryly for a man who nearly a year earlier had been told he had terminal cancer. He planned to work overtime that day.

By evening, hot pain was slicing through his back and hips and legs whenever the car hit a bump or pothole in the road.

Each time the slasher returned, my father said through gritted teeth, "Almost home."

He was passing the familiar houses of Pendleton. Suppertime had passed and children were spilling outside. But he longed to be inside. There the wives scrubbed kitchens pregnant with the reassuring odor of disinfectant and the muffled humming and splashing of automatic dishwashers. Stuffed with homemade food, the men tipped back in easy chairs and drank beer and whiskey and cheered as the Yankees belted home runs on television.

On Tonawanda Creek Road he counted three for-sale signs in front of ranch-style houses, reminders that heavy industry was leaving western New York. Tires humming over the steel grating of the bridge, the Volkswagen crossed the canal and onto Bear Ridge Road. He pressed down on the gas pedal. Mailboxes blurred. He wanted his wife and kids, a homemade meal, his comfortable easy chair, the rustle of the evening newspaper, a warm beer, the enchantment of television, more beer, more beer, sleep. He wanted the life he had known.

For most of that spring and summer, the cabin wasn't enough. Dad said we needed a new house that wouldn't trouble Mom with repairs after his death, and even though it would saddle her with a larger mortgage, she approved of his decision. But my sisters and I were sentimental about our home and about our orchard where the new house would be built, and argued that instead of building a new house we should have the old one fixed up. Nonetheless, our parents had made up their minds. Faced with an ending, they desired a beginning. With

cheerful desperation, they chose a builder, lender, and construction plan. Our home was put up for sale, and our orchard
was doomed.

All one morning, Grandfather's chain saw coughed and
snarled and screamed. I heaved the cut cherry, plum, and
quince wood up into the big dumper of Grandfather's old truck,
and Dad dragged away the branches that were too small to become firewood. Except for a short lunch break, we worked
steadily. By three o'clock all that was left of the orchard, where I
had climbed trees and played hide-and-seek and eaten cherries,
were thin piles of coarse oily sawdust, small pieces of branches,
stumps bleeding sap, and a big pile of green firewood. While I
finished heaving the wood into the dumper, Grandfather sat on
his truck's rusty footboard and Dad on a sticky stump, drinking
Genny and discussing the heating qualities of cherry wood.

Dad asked the contractor if he could use summer help, and he
reluctantly hired the customer's kid at the minimum wage. I
who had never encountered a nail I couldn't bend or a board I
couldn't saw crooked.

On my first morning of work, I was ordered to level piles of
dirt and straighten the sides of the trenches. The contractor sat
in his truck and watched, no doubt expecting me to loaf and
whine. But eventually he shrugged and said, "Maybe you'll
work out." Then he drove off. At the end of the day, when he returned and saw how much I'd done and that I was still laboring
hard, he whistled and said, "Pretty good."

After the concrete foundation hardened, I mixed mortar and
carried it and cinder blocks to three bricklayers who wore steel-

tipped work boots, denim shorts, and heavy gloves, their broad sweaty backs deeply tanned and their baked faces prematurely wrinkled. Barely acknowledging me, they yakked about cars and sports and women and music and bars as they plopped down mortar, tapped blocks level, smoothed joints. After twelve hours of work, they sped off in their pickups without tossing me a good-bye.

At eight the next morning, I was unloading lumber and kegs of nails from a flatbed truck while the contractor and two groggy carpenters, sipping steaming coffee from Thermos cups, looked over a blueprint spread out on the open tailgate of a pickup. The contractor finished giving instructions and drove away, and one of the carpenters, the contractor's son, introduced himself as Larry and informed me that I was piling the lumber in the wrong place.

Then the other strode over, scowling, a hammer swinging like a six-shooter from his carpenter's belt, and said, "I hear you don't know a roofing nail from a thumbnail."

"Maybe."

"But I hear you can work hard."

"Maybe."

"Maybe you better. Because if you don't do the shit we tell you, somebody else's gotta. Like me, for instance. And you wouldn't wanna piss me off—would ya now?"

"Maybe."

He laughed, extended his hand, and said, "I'm Gary. How d'ya do, kid?"

I fetched tools and nails and lumber, carried bundles of shingles up ladders, and did my best to spike studs and nail down

plywood. All the while, the carpenters chattered as the bricklayers had. One afternoon, Larry shouted, "One! You guys see that?
I drove that spike with one swing."

"It was three swings. I saw."

"Bullshit! It was *one*. Mark, didn't I? Tell'm."

"You're asking him? He's still counting how many swings
it's taking him to drive that spike he's bending. What're you on
now, Mark, ten or eleven?"

"At least he can count. No wonder you think it took me
three swings. You don't even fucking know how to count."

Gradually, I learned to use a hammer, and one morning the
boss raised my pay by a dollar an hour and asked if I wanted to
work for him, on other houses, for the entire summer. I said yes.
And that evening as I showered, I was proud of my firm muscles and dark tan and bloody fingernails. Although I was saving
for college, I fantasized about buying a sports car.

The contractor parked his pickup close to the house, opened the
window, and cranked up the radio. He ordered us to put down
our tools and listen. We stood quietly as three astronauts—who
had eaten steak and eggs for breakfast, the radio announcer informed us—lifted off at 9:32 A.M. atop 7.7 million pounds of
thrust or, as the announcer put it, "the power of five hundred
thousand automobiles."

Then the boss started his engine, turned down the radio,
and yelled, "Some day you guys'll point to this house and say,
'That's what I was doing when man left for the moon.' "

On the Sunday afternoon when Americans landed on the
moon, I was leaned back in Dad's easy chair. He was sitting on
the couch with Mom and April. Kim was stretched out on the

carpet in front of the television, on her side, her head on a pillow. Buzz Aldrin and Neil Armstrong were descending in the spidery landing craft, their voices crackling into our living room from more than two hundred thousand miles away: *three hundred feet. Down three and a half, forty-seven forward. One minute, one and a half down, seventy. Altitude velocity light. Fifteen forward. Coming down nicely. Two hundred feet. Four and a half down, five and a half down. Nine forward. Seventy-five feet.* Kim sat up. *Looking good. Down one half. Six forward, sixty second lights on.* I leaned forward, pushing down the foot rest. *Down two and a half. Forward. Picking up some dust.* I stood up. *Big shadow. Four forward. Four forward drifting to the right a little. Down one half. Thirty seconds . . .* Kim stood. *Contact light. Okay, engine stopped. ACA at a descent. Mode control both auto. Descent engine command override off. Engine arm off, four thirteen is in . . . Houston. We, uh. Tranquility Base here. The Eagle has landed.*

Mom and Dad hugged and kissed, their eyes filling with tears.

For supper we ate sandwiches in the living room. And we were still there hours later, the television images jerky and over-exposed, the astronauts all shimmering light, like angels, as Armstrong, stepping onto gray ashen moon dust, said, his voice faltering, "One small step for man." He paused. "A giant leap for mankind."

Again my mother and father hugged. Then Mom kissed April, who was nearly asleep.

The rest of the family went to bed, but Dad and I stayed up late while the astronauts rested in *Eagle.* He was back in his usual chair and I was on the couch when he asked me, "Do you know who heads the Apollo program?"

"No."

"General Samuel C. Phillips. My grandfather who came over from Ireland was named Samuel. Do you think maybe the general is some kind of relative of ours?"

I laughed.

"They call him General Anonymous because nobody knows who he is. But do you know who General Anonymous really is? It's the poor dumb bastards like me working their asses off year after year for less than they're worth to keep their families going and who pay their taxes and love their country. It's our money and sweat walking around up there in all that gear and glory. That's who General Anonymous really is. And dumb bastards that we are, we're proud of it."

Later that night, standing at the edge of the backyard beyond the reach of the maples, I gazed upward. I tried to picture the astronauts up there, on the moon, on what Aldrin had described as "magnificent desolation." Without television, I couldn't do it. All I could picture were two fleas on somebody's chilly bare ass. I had moon gazed so many times during my boyhood, wondering if there was life on it or wishing I was sharing the view with a girl, but now moon gazing seemed ridiculous. Suddenly, I felt downcast. They had stolen the moon.

I could barely turn off the damn alarm. My hands were claws. In the bathroom I turned on the hot water faucet with my wrists and held my claws in the soothing heat until the sore stiff muscles relaxed enough for my fingers to uncurl. Only then could I aim while I peed and, at the breakfast table, grip my spoon.

By the end of the summer, I hated my job, the dull sweaty repetition of it. All day I dwelled on my stiff hands, sore back, heavy eyelids, the tedious driving of another nail, the many slow minutes until lunch break and quitting time.

Gradually, I lost the energy to limit or mask my tics while I labored.

"Hey, Mark, I hear your nickname in school is Blinky. That right?"

"Yep. And I hear yours was Donna."

"No wonder you can't hit a fucking nail. You blink too much. You need fucking glasses or something."

"But I can hit faces good enough."

"I'll believe that when it happens."

Despite my cranky weariness, I began staying up until one or two in the morning watching TV. Finally I understood why my father, even before the cancer, was often cross when he came home from work. And why he needed a cabin and new house. And why, drinking beer after beer, he stayed up so late watching television, stretching his life away from the power plant and all the way to the tidal sphere.

During one of my final nights in my childhood home, I was shaken awake by thunder. The windows rattled and rain pounded the roof and the maples in the front yard swished and scraped against the house, and I detected moaning, as if a ghost were rising to greet the storm. I slowly crept to the stairway, and heard Mom's voice. I hurried down to the kitchen and saw that she was sitting next to Dad on the living room couch. He was leaning forward, his elbows on his knees, his forehead resting on his palms. Their forms were dark, the room unlit except for the orange glow of his cigarette.

"What's wrong?" I asked.

Another moan rose through the darkness.

"Can I help?"

"Daddy's in pain. Go back to bed, honey."

Light and shadows leapt through the muggy house during the instant before more shaking thunder. April called out from her sleep. Kim rolled, bedsprings creaking. Back in my bed, I remembered a morning years earlier when he informed me that he would be giving me a brushcut that evening: I had waited until he had departed for work, and then, in the presence of Mom and Kim, had said, "I hope he dies." I wondered if they remembered, and if he had ever been told. And then I recalled that recent afternoon in May when he had wept for me. I rolled from my back onto my stomach and onto my back again, the sheet damp and gritty with guilt. Yet within minutes I was recalling that I would play varsity football in the fall, was in love with two girls, had been invited to a party, would be going to college in two years. The force of the years I might live pulled my thoughts ahead.

I fell asleep in the future.

The immediate future was a new house stinking of fresh paint and carpeting. When the move was complete, I felt as if I were entering a house for the first time after a longtime resident had died. Despite the furniture and appliances, hollowness filled every room. The bank had paid for the construction with the understanding that the sale of our old house, combined with the eventual redemption of a twenty-thousand-dollar life insurance policy, would pay off the mortgage. We all knew what it would take to collect on the policy.

On the site of our old orchard, the yard was treeless and the house became hot beneath the summer sun. As if we were guests in the home of stern and distant relatives, my sisters and I spent most of our first few days there fanning ourselves in the seclusion of our new rooms, making only a few short and cautious ventures into the bathroom and kitchen. My parents had their new house. They had their new beginning with walls free of smudges and gouges, but Dad's pain, during his first several nights in a bedroom where he had made no repairs, steadily worsened.

One night when Mom was asleep, he heard me still moving around in my bedroom and limped in to talk. He sat down on the bed and asked about my training for the coming football season. But it better distracted him from his pain if he was the one doing the talking, and so he soon changed the subject to the cabin he had started to build before he knew he had cancer. With the thick tongue of the heavily drugged, he talked about the work we would finish and animals we would hunt and trees we would plant.

Slowly and suddenly, forty-two acres and a cabin had become our past and our future.

Dad had to give up his dream of the cabin becoming his retirement home. Instead of adding another story in the style of a Swiss chalet, as he had planned, he enlisted my Uncle Fred and cousin Danny to help us construct a pitched roof over the flat-topped single-story cabin. Uncle Al built a porch. And Dad lined the outside of the fireplace heatilator with fire brick, then began the slow work of facing the brick with stone. I gathered stones from the creek bed, mixed mortar, and helped with the lifting. Dad did all of the chiseling, often while grimacing in pain, sparks and shards flying as steel cut rock.

He welded together a stainless steel grill that could be swung in and out of the fireplace, and even on hot summer evenings we cooked our dinner meat inside over hardwood embers. When full with food, we talked. One warm night when the embers were dying and we had every window open, he told me that he had long believed he would die of cancer. He explained that when he was a young boy his oldest brother had died of the disease, and after that he had felt that cancer was somehow inevitable. I asked him what kind of cancer his brother Sam had had. He fell quiet, staring into the graying embers, and I could see that he was reshaping a story, summoning and chiseling the past for his benefit as much as mine.

He was summoning Sam, whose headaches had become so frequent and severe that he could no longer work as a draftsman, and who broke the bad news to Barley. My grandfather said there must be a mistake, and Sam replied that he had been to two doctors and they had reached the same conclusion. Barley said, "You can get better. Can't you?"

Sam shrugged. "It's in my brain, Pop."

His moistening eyes fixed on the tabletop, Barley nodded, and said in a near whisper, "You'll get better." He stood and walked slowly to a cupboard and removed two beer mugs. Then Sam followed him down the cellar steps to a tapped barrel.

The next day, Barley went along to meet the surgeon who would perform the operation. They listened as the man with the long and unblemished fingers, sitting behind a big mahogany desk, explained the surgery. Finally he asked, "Do you have any questions?"

"No," said Sam.

"Me, either," said Barley. "But I just want you to know I've decided I'm gonna watch you operate."

"I beg your pardon?"

"That way you'll be sure to be careful."

From above, through a glass observation window in the floor, he watched with an armed hospital guard at his side. He saw the shaven scalp bright in the light. He saw as the searchers, locked out of the mosque, slowly and neatly cut through the wall and lifted away a section, and saw them slip into the gray interior that throbbed with watery music, where they curtsied and circled and led out with the utmost courtesy, what little of it they could, the intruder.

In our new house in Pendleton linked to all the others by power lines, our father-son relationship could seem to march beneath flashing headlines and to a moaning electronic beat. My father read the *Buffalo Courier-Express* during his lunch break at the plant, listened to radio newscasts during the bumper-to-bumper drives home, and limped into our house well versed in the national news. Then he swallowed another pill, ate supper if he was up to it, poured a mug of Genny, unfolded the *Evening News,* and switched on Walter Cronkite. He settled into his easy chair with a grimace and moan. During commercials, he studied me with tired suspicion.

He accepted J. Edgar Hoover's assertion that Communists were bankrolling the antiwar movement, and assumed they were bankrolling the women's liberation movement as well. A member of Nixon's "silent majority," he didn't paste patriotic stickers on the bumpers of his Volkswagen or pickup truck, write letters to the editor, telephone his congressman, or even fly an American flag. But as Nixon well knew, the pained silent majority had strong beliefs and voted as if swallowing a necessary but bitter pill.

Even his son had been brainwashed by the enemy. As part of my growing rebellion against the authority that controlled the length of my hair, I had shed my conservative patriotism as easily as a snake sheds its skin. I increasingly felt it was my duty to oppose all of my father's political beliefs. And without exactly saying so, I let him know that I considered myself his moral superior.

He particularly disapproved of the antiwar demonstrations on the college campuses, and so I passionately defended the students. The flag-burning college kids, in his opinion, were spitting on their grandfathers and fathers who had saved and bettered America with great sacrifice. I argued that the students were fighting for their country, just like the patriots at the Boston tea party. Hadn't he seen the police dogs and clubs and tear gas on the news?

"You call that fighting?" he said. "Their daddies will bail them out of jail, and if one of them gets hurt, he'll hire'm a lawyer and sue. That's what we do. Bail out our kids. Even if the kids try to tear everything down while dumb Daddy pays their way through school. Those college kids wave signs and take drugs and screw like rabbits in the dorms. Some fight. Your Uncle Al, he enlisted when World War Two started. He had a wife and baby back home. He almost lost his life. That's what you call fighting for your country—not waving Vietcong flags and burning your own."

In truth, I wasn't very political. I didn't talk politics with my friends, and all I read in the newspaper was the sports page. Arguing was my excuse for talking to my father at home in

Pendleton, where in the incandescent glare of the power plant our relationship was as confusing as a radio program broken continually by static. In Pendleton, we seldom had anything else to say to each other.

But one evening I did ask him if he would change anything about his life if he had it to live over. Without pausing, he replied, "No." I then asked another, malicious question: Suppose that the coal dust, fly ash, or welding fumes had caused his cancer, wouldn't he, if he had it to do over, go to college, try for a better job? "No. My friends work at the plant."

For English class I was reading *The Hairy Ape,* Eugene O'Neill's play about an uneducated, misled, and fanatically proud laborer named Yank, and I believed I had recognized my father in the play.

"You'd have different friends."

But then the man who had lost his prostate and testicles to the knives of surgeons, who took Darvon for pain in the inoperable places, who was still welding at the plant, my father, smiling mischievously, gave a softly spoken reply uncharacteristic of a Yank: "Well, there is one thing I'd change. I would have raised you different."

On Sunday morning of Columbus Day weekend, we had nearly reached the cabin when he looked over at me and said, "Maybe I would. Maybe I would go to college."

I was startled out of near sleep in the bouncing cab of the pickup. We had exchanged only a few words, and those were at the start of the long ride. "What?"

"You asked me if I'd go to college if I had it to do over. Maybe I would. I could have gone nights instead of working overtime.

Maybe I would. I'd go into teaching. Done at three o'clock every day, Christmas and Easter vacations, summers off."

"Oh." The heater fan whirred. The morning sun was warm on my face, but through the cool glass I could see that the tomato and bean vines had been withered by frost. Beyond the brown gardens and big white farm houses, the tan corn stretched across the valley to the hills that rose scarlet and yellow into the blue and white sky.

"Imagine having the whole summer off."

"I do have the summer off."

"Well, yeah. But your whole life."

"I guess." I leaned back on the seat and closed my eyes again.

But he kept talking. "You should think about it. Going into teaching. Have you given it any thought, what you're gonna do?"

"Some."

I felt the lurch of the downshift on the steep hill into Ischua.

"Think about the time off, too."

I didn't reply. It was the only way to stop this conversation about my distant, distant future.

The block walls and concrete floor of the cabin still held the cold of the previous night. While Dad built a fire, I hiked the property so that I could be out in the sunshine. Beyond the pond, there was not much to see: a brook and spring, the stand of pine, a few hardwood trees, and a long strip of thorn and apple trees. The remainder of the forty-two acres was weedy. I could see from one end of the property to the other. A fox bounded out of the weeds and into the thorns with its red tail floating behind like the past trailing the future.

When I arrived back at the cabin, the fire was roaring and Dad was oiling his double-barrel shotgun. He was feeling well enough to hunt grouse, and soon, with a halting pace designed to unnerve the birds into sudden, whirring flight, we were hiking through the brushy portion of our land. We crossed the property line where faded orange surveyor's flagging still fluttered in the breeze, hunted through a hardwoods, and then crossed a paved road to reach a narrow meadow threaded by a small clear creek and sided by steep forested hills, iridescent in the rays of the still-climbing sun. There he killed the first grouse that flushed, and then I missed the next two. "Don't worry about the brush," he said. "You can't look for an opening— they're too fast. Just swing and shoot. Right through the brush."

But still I missed the next, final flush.

We hiked downstream until we found the beaver dam that Farmer Brown had told Dad about. Dad explained that the ravine was named Farwell Gulch after the first permanent settler in what would become the town of Ischua. And that beaver, which had been trapped out of the Alleghenies long before Farwell's arrival, were just beginning to return to the region. He told me that Farwell and other men had cut virgin white pine off these hills and with teams of horses had sledded the logs to Ischua Creek and then floated them to the Allegheny River, where they were lashed together into huge rafts and ridden all the way to the lumber mills of Pittsburgh.

The meandering base of the bright hills became increasingly steep, and eventually the creek swept against a cliff and dropped over a small falls in the shade of hemlocks clinging to shale. I nearly said I wished he'd bought land like this. But when I turned to speak, I saw that he was grimacing and rubbing his lower back with his left hand.

Even with me carrying both shotguns, it took him nearly two hours to limp back to the cabin.

After medication softened his pain in the late afternoon, he came outside to watch as I used his bamboo fly rod to pull a trout from the pond. He told me to leave its head on so that the pink flesh would be sweet, and later we cooked the fish along with our burgers over the fireplace flames.

As we ate, I realized something.

"We didn't do any work today."

"Nope."

"So what's tomorrow? Fireplace?"

"Nope."

"Finish the paneling?"

"Nope."

"What?"

"Same as today."

"What?"

"Nothing."

"Nothing?"

"Nothing."

"No work?"

In reply he asked if he had ever told me "The Story of the James Phillips Who Fell." I wanted to say, "Oh, God, have you ever." But I actually said, "I think you did once. He fell."

But he told me again.

I learned that a girl I secretly loved had started to date a boy I didn't like. That evening, Dad came home from work tired and hurting, and soon we were arguing about my hair. It was over my ears: why did I want to look like a girl?

"Because I've always wanted to be a girl. Is that what you want me to say? Now leave me alone."

"If you can't get a haircut when you need one, I'll start giving you brushcuts again."

"I'm old enough to grow my hair how I want."

"Not as long as you live under my roof."

"Then the hell with that. I won't live under your roof."

I went up into the kitchen, with Dad limping furiously behind, and called my friend Chuck Mullen and told him what had happened and asked if I could stay at his house. Dad went into his and Mom's bedroom.

While I waited on the line, my friend talked it over with his mother.

And even though Chuck was already sharing a small bedroom with his three brothers, she said yes. Chuck's parents were divorced and he was forever moving back and forth between their homes, and had lived in a couple of other places as well. So I supposed that his mother figured he and I wouldn't be staying long.

I yanked a few plastic trash bags from a box in the pantry. While I was emptying my closet and stuffing the clothing into the bags, Mom padded into my room. And though she already knew, she asked me what I was doing.

Instead of replying to her question, I reminded her that I didn't take drugs and was doing okay in school and had never been in trouble with the law. And I asked, "Isn't that good enough for him?"

She ignored my question and said, "Doesn't it matter to you that Daddy is dying?"

"You see—you guys must think I'm some kind of freak. Yeah—it matters. Of course it matters. But it has nothing to do with this."

"Can't you just do this for him? He's dying. He's in a lot of pain. He's still working for us. Can't you do this for him? It's just your hair he wants you to cut. That's all."

"No. I can't."

"Please."

"No."

She sighed, then turned away. She quietly closed the door behind herself. Then I sat down on the edge of my bed, my elbows on my knees and head in my hands. I was full of guilt, but I couldn't get the girl and her long-haired bastard of a new boyfriend out of my mind, and again my anger surged. I stood up and resumed stuffing the trash bags.

Without knocking, Dad opened the door. He said, "Put your clothes away."

"No, Dad. I can't."

"Yes, you can. You can grow your hair as long as you like. Grow it down to your ankles if you want. You're still my son."

He sat down on my bed, and I sat down next to him.

He said, "They cut my balls off."

For a few seconds, I sat there trying to understand. Was he speaking figuratively?

"What do you mean?"

"The doctors. When they did the surgery. When they took out the prostate. They took my balls, too."

I felt my scrotum contract.

"You had cancer there, too?"

He explained the reason for the surgery. And he told me that his testicles were replaced with plastic balls so that he would look normal in the shower room at the plant. But he could no longer have sex. Then he said, "At first I was gonna say no. I was gonna die with my balls, even if it was fast. But then I thought: What's the brave thing to do when I got a wife and three kids? The brave thing to do was to go ahead and get the operation."

Neither of us knew Freud from Frankenstein, but in a roundabout way Dad had just explained part of why we had fought about my hair. And we both knew it.

I sat there looking down at the rug, nodding. All I could say was "I'm sorry."

He stood slowly, with a quiet groan. He bent down and kissed me on the top of my head. He kissed my hair.

On Saturday, I borrowed the car and drove to the barbershop.

He chattered to drown out the call of pain. On a cold November afternoon, he and I were traversing the Alleghenies in his bouncing pickup as he talked about an Ulster landscape, of spring on his great-grandfather's farm—the setting of tales that my father had heard from his father, and that his father had heard from his father. I suspected Dad of confusing spring in southwestern New York with spring in Ireland, but I was glad he had given me a reason to recall the green months. Snow had yet to fall and remain, but winter had settled into the Alleghenies, and everything above the soil seemed brittle: the glazed puddles and tan corn stalks and bare trees and the nervous deer that soon would be shot. And so I longed for spring in the Alleghenies while my father spoke longingly of Irish hillside pastures in a thousand shades of green and of stony soil and of a gushing spring where in cold sweetness swam fairies who cached gold dust and played jokes on the Phillips children who came to fetch drinking water.

Several miles before we reached the cabin, Dad's face tightened and he leaned to his left, his right buttock lifting slightly off the pillow on the seat. When that didn't ease the worsening pain, he told me to get a Darvon capsule from the glove compartment. After he produced enough saliva, he placed the pill on his tongue and gulped. Then he said, "Talk to me."

"What?"

"Talk."

My mind raced: I wasn't especially interested in Ulster or the Welsh-Irish history of our family, the high school football season was over, our political discussions were like playing catch with a firecracker, and we had already talked about the Buffalo Bills and hunting.

"I wonder if it'll snow," I said.

"I hope so. Guys'll get cold and start tracking. Move the deer around better."

"That's what I was thinking, too."

Neither of us spoke for several more miles, and then he took one hand off the steering wheel to rub his eyes, and said, "I didn't want to take that pill until we were to the cabin. I'm already tired and it's not even in my system yet."

"You want me to drive?"

"We're almost there."

"I heard you last night. You know, in pain."

He nodded. Then he winced as he downshifted and pressed the brake pedal. The pickup was descending the long hill into Ischua, where we would turn off the main highway. In the distance we could see the corner store, fire hall, a church spire, and, rising beyond the last of the gaping old homes, a steep mountainside gray and brown with leafless forest.

Inside the cabin, we could see our breath. I crumpled newspaper and set it on the grate, added kindling and bigger pieces of wood, poured kerosene over the pile, and struck a match. From the chimney the thick white smoke swept down the roof, and through the window I saw it swirl around the yard before it suddenly rose through an opening in the pine canopy. When the fire was crackling, I went outside to unload the truck, whiffing wood smoke in the swirling breeze.

From the hose that channeled a portion of the flow close to the cabin, I collected springwater. When I came back inside with the two spilling pails, Dad was already asleep on the foldout couch, a bottle of pills and a bottle of whiskey on the floor near his empty boots. The sun was setting but I didn't light the propane lamps. I threw more wood on the fire, and then sat down in a big and lumpy stuffed chair that he had bought at a yard sale. I watched him sleep as the wood crackled and popped, light and shadows licking his face. He began to snore. I tiptoed over to the couch. There were deep circles under his eyes but otherwise his face was still youthful. His pained legs had become sticks and even his arms were withering. But he was growing a potbelly. I took two swallows of whiskey.

Sitting in the chair, whiskey warmed, I watched the yellow flames shooting up into the chimney until they shrank into a blue hissing and crumbled into orange and red. Out on the dark lawn coarse with numbing frost, barefoot, I peed. Back inside, I heaped on more logs and changed into pajamas and slid into a sleeping bag on the lower bunk and smiled at the thought of fairies, a clan of imps, swimming in our spring.

We had just wiggled out of our sleeping bags when Grandfather flung open the cabin door and said, "I don't smell any breakfast cooking. Where's my eats?"

Standing near the fireplace embers, still wearing the clothing he'd fallen asleep in, his eyes red and lids puffy, Dad said, "We got tired of waiting for you. Got up at dawn and ate breakfast, just like always. Fed yours to the raccoons."

"Up?" Grandfather laughed. "Up my ass. You guys slept in awful late. You musta gone out with some hillbilly girls last night."

While Dad fried breakfast on the propane stove, I helped Grandfather empty his pickup cab. "Lookit all this stuff my wife sent along," he said. "Must be she doesn't want me to come back."

Dad wasn't feeling well and stayed inside, but after breakfast Grandfather and I went fishing in the pond. Using a freshly cut branch for a pole and worms for bait, he caught three rainbow trout; using Dad's fly rod and a streamer, I caught nothing. We then hiked through open woods and through an abandoned apple orchard overgrown with weeds and briars, checking the mast and fruit crops and searching for deer beds and trails. When we returned to the cabin, our red woolen coats covered with burrs, we were happy to see that Dad was feeling better, had cold beer and pop waiting on the table, and was frying the pink trout fillets.

After lunch, Dad tuned in the Bills' game on the radio. For much of the afternoon, he and I cheered and moaned and punched the air, and during halftime talked about my high school team and the days when Dad played in an amateur league and was known as Crazy Legs Phillips.

As for Grandfather, the only "sport" he followed was phony wrestling. Anyhow, he was constitutionally unable to sit for longer than an hour. He stayed outside during most of the game, and I heard the two-count ripping of a hand saw, pounding and tapping, the shrieking of a chain saw, the brief roar of his pickup motor, the sharp slamming of the truck and porch doors.

After we washed and dried the supper dishes, Dad and Grandfather played penny poker and I listened to fragments of their hunting stories while tending the fire and reading deer-hunting articles from the two dozen old outdoor magazines that Dad had bought at the same yard sale as the stuffed chair. Before going to bed we oiled our guns and located our ammunition and knives and compasses and hunting licenses and lengths of rope and laid out our red woolen hunting coats and pants and hats and gloves and socks and our long underwear and flannel shirts and insulated boots and remembered to stuff chocolate bars and hard candy and toilet paper into the pockets of our coats and pants. As he climbed into the top bunk, Grandfather said, "You better not put much wood on that fire, Markie. It's plenty warm up here already."

Nonetheless, I hoped I wouldn't need to get out of bed to tend the fire before morning, and so around midnight, after I stopped reading and spread my sleeping bag on the couch, I heaped five logs of ironwood atop the deep embers.

As the windup alarm clock finished clanging, I stumbled over something sizable on the cabin floor. The fireplace embers were barely glowing and the cabin was dark. Suddenly wide awake, I located a flashlight on the fireplace mantel and swept the beam over the floor, and saw my grandfather stretched out on an open sleeping bag, his pajamas and underwear shed.

"Why are you on the floor?"

With his forearm shielding his eyes from the beam of light, he asked, "Didn't you get awful hot in the night?"

"No."

He laughed. "When you cook breakfast, just make the eggs and toast. Forget the bacon, Markie. We got plenty. Because last night it got so hot up on that top bunk, my ass fried."

From the lower bunk, Dad said, "I'm glad to know it was sweat dripping down on me, George. I thought you pissed the bed."

"It would have evaporated before it got to you."

I fried the eggs and bacon, and toasted the bread, balanced on a fork, above the blue flame of the stove. While Dad and I were still on our first helping, Grandfather said, "I need more eats." So I finished eating while standing, frying more eggs and bacon. Grandfather still finished in time to beat Dad and me into the woods before the sun rose.

It was my second season of hunting deer, but I had yet to realize that it is more important for a deer hunter to be knowledgeable about the other hunters in the woods than it is for him to be knowledgeable about deer. If a hunter knows how to stay warm and the location of the other hunters, how long they can sit in the cold, and where they will walk after they become cold, he will be sitting while they are not and might see one of the deer they will flush. At dawn I sat down on a stump within shooting distance of a stream, a rutted deer trail, and the intersection of a beech woods and overgrown apple orchard. But no deer came to eat fallen fruit or nuts or to drink. They were hiding from the hunters they'd seen, scented, and heard entering the woods at dawn.

Within two hours I was shivering and tried stalking, but the crunching of frozen leaves announced my approach. And soon gunfire was repeatedly echoing through the hills as freezing stalkers such as myself unintentionally chased deer to the hunters who were yet sitting.

I saw only one living deer all morning, the white underside of its raised tail undulating as it bounded away. And soon after the deer was out of my sight, a shotgun boomed, causing me to jump.

Hurrying in the direction of the shot, I came upon Grandfather standing over a buck. He looked up, laughed, and said, "You make a good deer hound, Markie."

As I helped him roll the deer onto its back, he said, "You might as well learn how to gut a buck."

I had never gutted anything larger than a rabbit, but once I had watched Grandfather skin, disembowel, and saw apart a steer. And so without waiting for his instructions, I unsheathed my knife and inserted the point beneath the deer's skin where the rib cage began to separate into two sections. I cut toward the tail, careful to keep the blade below the skin and above the entrails, the full stomach and gray coiled intestines bulging through the opening.

"Pretty good job. Now cut off the balls and I'll show you a trick."

I did as he said.

Then he ran his knife around the anus and tied it off with a length of boot lace: "Now when the guts come out, the asshole will come loose with everything else and no shit will leak on the meat."

I paused, hoping he would finish the job, but he instructed me to remove my coat, roll up my shirtsleeves, and reach up into the chest to sever the wind pipe and esophagus. While I followed his instructions, he quickly removed the floppy liver and firm heart and put them in a large plastic bag that he had pulled from his coat pocket. My hands and arms sticky with blood, we rolled the deer back onto its side. I reached through the steaming guts to the backbone and worked the remaining organs free, easing them out onto the leaves as one mass. Grandfather wedged the cavity open with a stick, to cool the flesh, then filled out the "kill tag" portion of his hunting license and tied it onto one of the small antlers with boot lace. I tied one end of my drag rope around the other antler, pulled on my coat, and we began to drag the carcass out of the woods, leaving a trail of hair and blood on the roiled leaves.

Grandfather had driven home to butcher his deer, Dad could hunt for merely an hour or so before pain forced him to leave the woods, and I had become discouraged. Dad wanted a buck to be hanging from the meat pole when Mom and my sisters arrived on Thanksgiving, but though he gave me detailed hunting advice before sunup, I was too restless to sit on a stump near the deer trail he had suggested. Instead I tracked deer over hills now covered with snow, and spotted squirrels, birds, other hunters—but no deer.

Then late in the afternoon, when falling snow was tickling my neck, an old buck stood up from a bed concealed by briars, his massively antlered head held high and ears flicking and a front paw slicing the snow as I happened to look up from his large white tracks. He spun and leapt over a tangled deadfall before the butt of the gun was halfway to my shoulder. I cursed. Then I turned and followed my own tracks, which were filling with snow, back to the cabin.

The snowstorm was spent by the next morning when I left the cabin. I sat down on a stump, in a location that Dad had suggested, and soon was squinting in the white glare as the sun rose in the blue sky above the leafless woods.

I periodically closed my eyes, resting them. Loosened by the heat, clumps of snow swished off branches and landed with faint thumps, and once I momentarily detected the soft crunching of snowy stepping, but I was nearly asleep and told myself that the sound was just more falling snow, and didn't open my eyes. At noon I stood and stretched, turned, and spotted footprints. Someone had walked within thirty yards of my back. I could see that he had stood there for some time: had lit an L&M cigarette, tossed the match, smoked, tossed the butt, and left. I followed his tracks back to the cabin.

He asked, "See any deer?"

"Nope."

"That's funny. I could have sworn I heard one snorting somewhere around where I told you to sit."

"No. Didn't see a thing. You see anything?"

"Nope. At least no deer."

In darkness we ignored the alarm clock and stayed in our sleeping bags until late in the morning. I was to meet Mom and my sisters at noon, and after a late breakfast I pulled a long toboggan, supporting a narrow wooden box, out the driveway and up the steep hill of the unplowed dirt road.

Near the intersection of our road and a plowed road, in the kitchen of his old house sided with asphalt roofing, I waited with Will, my father's cranky friend and neighbor in Ischua. The house was filled with the odors of wood smoke and roasting turkey. On a paper plate centered on the plastic tablecloth, a pool of white grease had coagulated around the bacon left over from breakfast. As usual, Will was pissed off. Like the truck driver he once was, he spit maledictions for forty minutes—at the president, governor, town supervisor, county highway department, school board, various neighbors, the weather, hunters who shoot from cars, the doctor who was treating his arthritic hip, and teenagers who drive too fast. Playing with a toy truck on the kitchen floor, in a quiet singsong, his grandson imitated the litany: "Ga dan ga dan. Son a bit. Bass are. Ga dan son a bit bass are."

After the tinny beeping of the Volkswagen's horn rescued me, Will and I transferred the food and a suitcase from the car to the box on the toboggan. April climbed on behind the box, and Mom and I gripped the pull rope and began the haul down the road, over drifts broken by windswept gravel. Will gave Kim a lift on his snowmobile, and as they dipped from view into the brushy ravine below the cabin, I could hear the engine's sputtering and Will's cursing.

Mom had cooked the pumpkin pie and the turkey the previous day. When I went out to help Kim shovel off the pond for skating, the stuffed turkey was warming in the propane oven and Mom was peeling potatoes. The previous night, wind had swept almost all of the snow off the ice, polishing the pond so smooth that it was difficult to keep our footing while shoveling the remaining snow. Now there was no wind and it was sunny, and the noise in the hills told me that the local farmers were conducting their traditional Thanksgiving deer drive, the younger men shouting and howling as they hiked toward the older men on post.

Kneeling on the pond, Kim tied on her white skates while I sat on the end of the dock. Because the ice was thin, she was wearing a life jacket. As she started skating, her ankles turned in but she straightened them and gained speed until she neared the opposite bank of the pond and fell as she tried to turn. She got up laughing in the bright orange life jacket. In the hills, the pincher was closing and the gunfire was almost constant. When Kim had been skating for some time, Dad opened the cabin door, stuck two fingertips into his mouth, and whistled us in for dinner. Then he leaned out farther to listen. He yelled, "Sounds like we should be in the woods!"

Dad said grace, and as we all lifted our heads, Mom said, "I think we should each give thanks for something. I'll start. I'm thankful we can all be together this Thanksgiving."

Kim said, "I'm thankful we can all be together this Thanksgiving."

April said, "Me, too."

It was my turn. I had planned to say I was thankful for the food, but Mom's thanks, with its suggestion that the day was approaching when we wouldn't be together, unnerved me. I couldn't speak.

Mom gasped faintly.

Kim stared at me angrily.

And Dad said, "I'm thankful we're all together."

They wanted to hack away some more of him. Because adrenaline helped feed the tumors, his doctors wanted to remove both of his adrenal glands; they were also proposing treatment with an experimental drug that might slow the spread of the disease. But the drug reacted toxically with alcohol. Dad said to me, "I don't know if it's worth it, giving up beer just to get an extra year or two. Just *maybe* to get an extra year or two."

Late one night, I woke thinking that a gale had come up, when actually I was hearing Dad's moaning. And in the morning, he decided that he would take the pills and consider the surgery.

He was also considering something else.

And instead of keeping the pistol under the bed as he had in the days following the removal of his prostate and testicles, he kept it within easier reach, in the drawer of the nightstand abutting his side of the bed. After one of his doctors told my mother that Dad had brought up the subject of suicide, she informed the doctor about the gun, and he urged her to hide it. She did as the doctor wanted, but left Dad's two shotguns in their bedroom closet: somehow it was understood that just as a hand saw is for cutting wood and a hack saw for metal, the shotguns were for hunting and the pistol for self-destruction. When Dad noticed that the pistol was gone, he said to Mom, "So you're gonna let them take that away from me, too?"

It was returned to the nightstand.

After football season was over, I began to spend time with boozers; while my father was learning to do without beer, I was learning to like it too much. My new buddies bought cases of

Schlitz from a corner store that competed with the supermarkets by selling alcohol to minors, and we began our evenings by drinking in snowy town parks or along secluded stretches of railroad tracks. I told myself that I was soothing the pain and worry of my home life. I imitated my buddies, who drunkenly brayed, cursed at the top of their lungs, and fought other boys or one another if girls were along.

Still working full-time, Dad was too pained and wearied to keep track of what I was doing with my spare time. And because our new house was a split-level with my bedroom on the lower floor and my parents' on the upper, I could enter from an evening of binging without my family noticing that I was staggering and smelled of beer. Sometimes I stood for a moment on the landing and listened for moaning, but as often as not I heard only the television and the laughter of my sisters.

After dinner Dad took a pain pill and limped to his bed, and my sisters and mother joined him in watching the news and shows on the portable television that sat on the dresser. Exhausted from waking so often at night, baggy-eyed Mom usually fell asleep soon after the evening newscast was over. Sitting on a bedside chair, Kim worked with practiced cheer at distracting Dad from his pain while commercials were on. Sometimes he let April stay up late to watch *Hee Haw, Get Smart, The Courtship of Eddie's Father, The Jim Nabors Hour, Laugh-In*. He and my sisters watched dramas, too, but never *Medical Center* or *Marcus Welby, M.D.* It was later at night, in darkness, when the family had split up, that the pain prevailed—and the nightstand drawer was opened and closed, opened and closed, opened and closed.

I had convinced myself that I wasn't missed while I was out drinking. But one night Kim knocked on my bedroom door and asked where I'd been. Without opening the door I replied that it was none of her business. Then she asked, "Do you think you could stay home tomorrow night? I got the home movies out of the attic."

I thought for a moment, then said, "If nothing else comes up."

The next evening, Dad set up the screen and projector in the living room and removed several rolls of film from a cardboard box. For over two hours, our new house darkened except for the screen colored with our past, we watched the honeymoon, babies sleeping and silently squealing, birthday parties, Christmas mornings, the vacation at Chautauqua Lake, a New Year's Eve party at which Dad became so drunk that he danced with another man, blind Grandma Phillips eating in the kitchen of our previous home, and especially my sisters and me playing and seeming to grow by the minute. Much of the action took place in or around water: Mom and Dad diving off a small cliff into a lake, Dad bathing in a lake and wading into a rushing stream and spraying Mom's younger sister with a hose, Mom watering flowers and water-skiing and fishing, me at age two spraying myself while trying to water Grandmother Wagner's garden, Kim skating on the pond.

When the lights were back on, Dad said, "All that water made me thirsty for a beer."

"Oh sure," said Kim. "You mean that wild New Year's party made you thirsty for a beer."

I said, "If you think you're gonna dance with me, forget it."

Late that night I woke to the sound of wrenching heaving. I found Dad kneeling in front of the toilet. Kneeling next to him, Mom was caressing his back. When he saw me, he said, "I had to have just one more beer; didn't I?"

I talked Mom into going back to bed and then I sat up with him, nervously chattering until his nausea passed an hour later. After he went into the bedroom, I sat at the kitchen table until I could hear his snoring.

Then I removed a bottle opener from a drawer, and walked into the laundry room where there was a case of Genesee that had been purchased weeks earlier. Sitting on a footstool, I guzzled bottle after bottle until I stood unsteadily, opened both faucets of the laundry sink, and vomited into the draining swirl.

On Easter morning, Kim asked that our family attend church. But I had stopped attending a month earlier, upsetting Mom, who had appealed to Dad for help. He had replied, "I don't go to church much myself. So how can I make him go if he really doesn't want to?"

But now he sighed resignedly, as if we had a family dental appointment. "You, too, Mark. Your sister really wants us all to go, for some reason. So we're all going. Now get changed into your good clothes."

The congregation had recently built a new church. I had liked the atmosphere of the old one: the creaking floor and scarred wooden pews made of virgin timber, the tonality of hymns sung under the high ceiling, the arching stained glass windows, the cold in January that made people want to sit close together. I had enjoyed imagining the prayers of a mother whose only son was a Union soldier in the Civil War, a farmer thankful for a big crop harvested with the help of draft horses, an insecure boy who wanted to ask a pretty girl to the barn dance, a young widower whose wife had died in childbirth. But in the new church, smelling of fresh paint and new carpeting, I found it difficult, sitting on a folding chair, to stop thinking of the well-dressed parishioners as customers and of the minister as an insurance salesman.

As we crossed the lawn toward the driveway, Kim whispered to me, "Every night I pray for God to make him better."

I almost laughed. But then I glanced over my shoulder at Dad, several steps behind us, shuffling. He was still sore from his latest operation and had been taking, as a substitute for adrenaline, a steady dosage of cortisone. The cortisone made it difficult for him to sleep even when he was exhausted and free of pain.

I shrugged. "Can't hurt."

While we were crossing the parking lot, the church door was opening and closing and we caught glances of the minister in the foyer greeting ladies wearing flowery hats and men in long suit coats and children in uncomfortable shoes. I pictured the minister fleeing our house after my father had flung open the bedroom door, and noticed that Dad was smiling for the first time all morning.

He picked up his pace, leading our family.

Like a rising tide, the goldenrod and briars and crab apples and poplar and pine and hardwoods were spreading across the abandoned farmland of the Alleghenies. One of our neighbors in Ischua witnessed a sow bear and two cubs cross the road less than a mile from the cabin; beavers dammed culverts and flooded the back roads; wild turkeys were heard gobbling from the hilltops for the first time in over a century.

Dad and I decided to go turkey hunting. We didn't take along a call; didn't know the proper way to hunt turkeys in the spring is to lure the toms by imitating the yelps and clucks of the hens. After we had walked some distance into the predawn woods, he whispered, "Sit here and hold still. They come here to eat. You'll see where they've scratched the leaves."

I did as he said, and after a tom had finished gobbling on its roost at dawn, it flew down and soon appeared where Dad had said one might. Later that morning, I set the dead bird on the scale at a hardware store and learned that it weighed twenty-three pounds. Three years would pass before I even saw another turkey, but for a time I believed that hunting wild turkeys was as easy as buying sliced turkey from a supermarket.

While he and I were working on the fireplace that afternoon, Dad told me how his great-grandfather had poached pheasants on the English estates in Ulster without firing a shot or setting an incriminating snare. At a secluded spot, William Phillips spread grain. He waited until several pheasants were feeding on the grain each morning, and then began spreading whiskey-soaked grain. After that he merely needed to seize the drunken birds and toss them into a sack.

"Sounds as easy as turkey hunting."

"Tell me if you still think so next year," he said. "If I'm still around."

Before it could be discovered by the nocturnal raccoons that would come to hunt salamanders, at dusk I walked to the spring to retrieve the turkey, plucked and eviscerated, from the cast-iron scalding kettle used as a cattle trough by an earlier owner of the property. The water table was high with snow melt and rain and the spring gushed around the big kettle, and before carrying the wrapped and chilled turkey to the cabin porch, I sat down on the thick arching root of the hollow ash. In the twilight, I listened to the cold rising and falling water murmuring over and over an indecipherable word.

On the tepid flow of summer we drifted into new routines. Dad learned to function with little sleep, swallowed Darvon on schedule, and left for work each weekday morning without complaint. Mom expected to be awakened several times each night by moaning and by the nightstand drawer opening and closing, opening and closing. She took a nap each afternoon, and still managed to cook meals and do laundry and keep the house immaculate. April played with Barbie dolls and her neighborhood friends, and remembered to sit close to Dad instead of on his aching lap. During the evenings when he was in pain, Kim continued trying to distract and cheer him. I kept him up to date on how much money I was earning at my new job as a stock boy, and even when he was in pain he nodded his approval.

Robins hunted hurriedly as the sun, yellow and floating now, began to draw up the dew and drive the worms into the soil. Lunch boxes swinging, hair damp and combed, men strode out of quiet homes, glanced at their watches, slammed car doors, cranked engines. Traffic sped up and down Bear Ridge Road.

Chuck Mullen drove his old Chevy into the driveway, honked twice, and I jogged out of my home clutching a bagged lunch.

Until I began my summer job at a department store in nearby Lockport, I supposed that the smiling clerks and cashiers—wearing neat uniforms and asking perkily, "May I help you?" and "Did you find everything?"—were happy to be cogs in a sales machine. But of course I soon realized that they had aching feet, were desperately bored, and that their smiles were mandated by management. And they weren't the only employees who hated their jobs: an assistant manager drank vodka on the job, and once at a staff meeting I heard the head manager explode: "Goddamn the customers! They pay with counterfeit money! Their checks bounce! They steal our merchandise! They filthy it with their grubby fingers!"

During one of my breaks in the coffee room, a salesclerk said to another, "You should have had the dream I had last night. I was putting price stickers on packages of panties and I hear this pounding and look up and here comes this hunk—it turns out to be John Wayne himself—charging up the lingerie aisle on a big white horse. I kid you not! I'm worried maybe I'm gonna find out he's a sicko. But it's not pink underwear he's after—it's me! Me! And he no sooner sweeps me off my feet than—shit—I wake up. I kid you not!"

She slapped her own face, once on each ample cheek, and added, "Now there's a man that melts my butter. Not like these little crook stock boys." She glanced at me with disgust. I wasn't a crook, but I understood why she assumed I was. Most of the stock boys regularly snuck merchandise down the loading ramp, stashing the loot in the Dumpster behind the store until they were off work.

Our wallets smoking with the money we had earned, Chuck and I spent our Friday nights at a nightclub in Lockport. The legal drinking age in New York was eighteen, but Chuck knew the bouncer. The club featured local rock bands, and from our seats we lustily watched the women dance with drunken wildness. Tapping our fingers on the tabletop and our heels on the floor, we pretended to enjoy the bad and deafening music. We drank pitchers of Canadian beer, but never worked up the nerve to ask anyone to dance. We stayed until around midnight, and then, drunk, he drove us home over back roads where he was unlikely to encounter the police.

Friday was my one night out, my only real extravagance. I was saving my money for college. I was filling most of my free time by training for football season, watching television with my family, reading college catalogs at my desk, or staring at the white ceiling above my bed as twangy folk songs spun from my record player, filling my room with regret and longing. I couldn't believe that I was about to become a senior. For the first time in my life, I was wondering where the days and years had gone. Maybe I really would go to college, get a permanent job, raise a family. Maybe my father really would die.

Dad's suggestion that I become a teacher was starting to make sense. Everyone seemed beaten down by their jobs—the welders, bricklayers, carpenters, clerks, cashiers, even the bosses. My summer jobs had made me feel like the rest of them. It was important to have time off. Teachers had time off.

I stored the college catalogs under my bed and contemplated their sales pitches while staring at the white ceiling of my bedroom as if it were a map of the future on which I could trace a route. By the end of July I had decided to attend Bloomsburg State College in Pennsylvania, to become an English teacher.

English was my best subject, Bloomsburg accepted students with C averages, and the campus was far enough but not too far from home.

On a sticky evening, in the middle of the front lawn beneath a wide maple with glossy leaves hanging still, Dad was briefly free of pain. He and I had fled the sweltering house and were sitting in metal lawn chairs and rocking slightly on the curved springy legs. Nestlings chirped and robins hopped across the lawn.

Throughout the neighborhood, men and children, and women after the kitchen work was done, all full with food, came outside. The adults sat in shaded lawn chairs or began washing and polishing cars in the driveways. Children in bathing suits ran shouting through the cool arching spray of lawn sprinklers, fell, and jumped up laughing with blades of grass sticking to their skin; my sisters migrated barefoot up the shoulder of the road, stepping gingerly on the gravel, to visit a neighbor who owned a small pool. The traffic was light, and in the house across the road Beverly Herd's flute blasted and lurched, and from somewhere else came muffled rock music and a DJ gabbing fast and then a sharp parental order before the radio was turned down to a fast undulating whisper.

I asked Dad if he would drive me to Bloomsburg so I could inspect the campus. He nodded. A moment later, he said, "Sure."

Without further talk, we sat in our lawn chairs until my sisters returned as dusk thickened into night and the living room windows of the neighborhood filled with yellow light.

It was that time of year in the Alleghenies when it is autumn in the mornings and summer in the afternoons. Driving until daylight, Dad pulled the car off the road near a weigh station on Pennsylvania Route 15. While he switched seats I climbed out, stretched, breathed deeply. The light angled over the mountains, irradiating the yellow tips of the roadside goldenrod while the stems and leaves remained tucked in shadows, and birds winged south in a silent flock. Gathering mist rose off ponds and streams and the peaks of the higher mountains were obscured in it. The top of the puttering Volkswagen was damp. My urine pooled around a rear tire. A tractor trailer blasted by, shaking the car as I climbed into the driver's seat and pulled the door shut.

In the still towns where the green bridges were rusty and the red brick walls were sooty and there were many gin mills and signs for yard sales and rooms for rent, everything seemed to complain of the closing coal mines and steel mills and the oil wells gone dry. Between the towns, where the highway snaked and dipped steeply, the signs and billboards blurred by through the mist: AMERICAN TRUCKSTOP FAMILY RESTAURANT, WEST'S DELUXE HOTEL, ENDLESS MOUNTAIN REAL ESTATE, COVINGTON COMMUNITY CENTER, GINNY BLACK'S BEAUTY SALON, SUR-LOC STORAGE, WILD TURKEY FARM MARKET, TEXACO, PRODUCE FOR SALE, PEACHES— CORN—CUCUMBERS—TOMATOES, WOOLWORTH CHIROPRACTOR, KING- DOM PRINTING, GOLDEN RULE LUMBER, STEAM VALLEY RESTAURANT, WILSON'S CHEVROLET, MOUNTAIN VIEW RESTAURANT, COUNTRY ROOSTER ANTIQUES AND GIFTS, MATT'S AUTO PARTS, HEMLOCK MOTEL, REDUCED GEAR ZONE, FALLING ROCKS, FEAR OF THE LORD IS THE ROAD TO SALVATION, TOWN OF LIBERTY: PERMITS REQUIRED.

Near Trout Run the mountains rose higher and I leaned forward and glanced up through the top of the windshield to see the forested peaks rolling into one another far above the blurred

outcrops of red rock squeezing the highway where dead opos-
sums, raccoons, and deer lay mangled on the gravelly shoulders
lined with stunted and crooked sumac. Now and then the
Susquehanna River came into view far below, sweeping grayish
around a green misty mountainside.

Dad rode with his eyes closed, moaning faintly, and until he
fell asleep I spoke to him about football and my summer job and
the scenery. By the time the sun was high and the mountains had
stretched out and the hemlock and hickory had given way to
brown-tasseled corn and cut clover, we were nearing my chosen
college.

We checked into a motel near the edge of town. Dad had
planned to take a side trip to a coal-mining museum, but he was
in too much pain and too drugged. He lay on the bedspread, on
his back, his eyes closed, smoking cigarettes. I watched television for a time, then tried to nap but couldn't with my future so
near.

Later that afternoon we rode into Bloomsburg, which was
like none of the other towns we'd passed through in Pennsylvania. It seemed ablaze with bookstores, bicycle and ski and clothing shops, movie theaters, florists, a jeweler, an art gallery, fra-
ternity and sorority houses, places to eat. Students wearing
backpacks rode bicycles, weaving around small parked cars,
and on the sidewalks others held hands, window-shopped,
yelled greetings to friends on opposite sidewalks. I caught a
smoky whiff of marijuana.

We ate lasagna in the booth of a small Italian restaurant with
a juke box that played folk and rock. Then we began the hike up
the main street toward the campus where we could see, above

the maples of College Hill, the brass dome of the clock tower, golden in the rays of the dipping sun. It was six o'clock and the tower bonged and chimed. I said, "That's beautiful." I began walking faster.

"Slow down."

I stopped and waited for him to catch up. We stood side by side, looking up at the dome until he stopped panting. Then he said, "You go ahead. I don't think I can make it. I'll wait in the car. Take as long as you want."

He turned around and began limping down the hill. For the first time since I had conceived of our trip to Bloomsburg, it struck me that this was practice for what would happen a year later, if he should still be alive.

"Dad!"

He turned around and I stepped quickly downhill and threw my arms around him. He was surprised and I held on for so long that he must have wondered if I would ever let him go.

The class of 1971 was herded into the funnel. There we fought to stay awake during aptitude testing, flipped hurriedly through guides to careers, and were wooed by school-to-school salesmen selling colleges. Our fretful parents had seen in the American dream that each generation must receive a longer and more expensive education than the previous, and to them the guidance office provided forms for college loans. We seniors were asked over and over, "What do you plan to do with your life?"

Pete Venezia intended to play lead guitar in a rock band, Melissa Strout to act on Broadway, Blinky Phillips to have a lot of time off. But like the rest of our classmates, we told the anxious adults what they wanted to hear. I said, "I wanna be a English teacher."

My guidance counselor nodded his approval, leafing through his file on me. "I see you're taking trigonometry and chemistry this year. How are you doing so far in those?"

"Great," I lied.

"You'll need to pass them to stay on the college track. Even to be an English teacher."

I almost said, "If I don't get drafted and end up in Vietnam." But by then the war was ending, and I knew that the damaged cartilage in my left elbow, which I'd dislocated years earlier while broad jumping in gym class, would keep me out of the army. And so like the rest of my classmates, I simply said, "Yes."

To all of his urgings, yes.

The rebellious sixties had arrived late and mild in Pendleton. We teens danced to the Stones and Beatles, to the beat of millionaires, and made fashion statements by quoting Bob Dylan and Janis Joplin in term papers. And the growing popularity of illegal drugs merely signified that alcohol was no longer the sole intoxicant of style. Boys grew their hair longer and some of the girls went braless, but we were still herded into the funnel, in our stylish disguises.

I wore the ubiquitous faded blue jeans and tie-dyed T-shirts and low-top sneakers, but kept my hair fairly short. Other than alcohol, I refused to use any drugs, which I associated with pain and cancer. I stayed home while my friends, laughing and popping pills and smoking reefer and hollering to be heard over the vibrating radio speakers, journeyed in a crowded car to a rock concert in Buffalo or Niagara Falls.

I had been elected captain of the football team, had friends, and possessed the normal sexual drive of an eighteen-year-old boy, but I began to stay home more and more. I stopped attending so-cial events at school, and even though I was of the legal drinking age, I seldom accompanied my friends to Brauer's Tavern, Pendle-ton's watering hole. Chuck accused me of becoming a hermit.

The problem was that it had become difficult for me to live in the present without worrying about the approach of doom. I enjoyed thinking about a disconnected future, about a life away from home, but couldn't imagine a different present. It was the fourth year of Dad's cancer, and increasingly, pressingly, the present wasn't for parties and school dances and girlfriends. It was for my father's dying. The experimental medication had halted the spread of the cancer for the time being, but the tu-mors were still there, waiting—and were only so patient. The pain was still there. Like dammed water, eventually the disease would trickle and rush past artifice, and like the little Dutch boy with his finger in the dike, I didn't travel much.

During my entire senior year, I went on only one date.

I was playing ticktacktoe with the champion of study hall, and immediately after she permitted me to win a game, I let it slip out: "Would you wanna go out sometime?"

When I arrived to pick up Linda, her mother asked me my father's first name, how old he was, and where he had grown up. She said she believed he was the same Jimmy Phillips she had dated for several months when she was a girl in Buffalo, and added, "You sure look like him. He was awful good-look-ing." And then, "Well, you two have a nice time now."

Outside, I said, "That was easy."

"My mom's nice."

We watched a high school basketball game, then went to a pizza parlor. I tried not to talk about myself because there was always a chance that once I got started I would tell the full truth. And so instead I encouraged Linda to talk about herself. During the drive home she said, "Usually boys just like to talk about themselves." Then she reached over and placed her left hand on my right leg above my knee. Big wet snowflakes were falling, the wipers were swishing, the heater fan was humming. I was warm and happy, sitting next to a pretty and kind girl, her hand on my thigh.

Her long driveway hadn't been plowed. Twice the Volkswagen nearly became stuck. I had never before driven in a snowstorm and was worried about becoming stuck or somehow damaging Dad's car. I began to blink rapidly, and when we reached the end of the driveway, I said, "I'm kind of worried about getting home in this weather, so would it be okay if we kissed good night in the car instead of walking you in?"

"Sure."

The house was dark, her family in bed. I leaned past the stick shift and over the narrow space between the bucket seats and we touched lips and tongues. Gradually I leaned farther into the passenger seat and slowly my left leg straightened and my left foot eased off the clutch pedal until suddenly the car, still running and in second gear, lurched forward and met the garage door with a loud shuddering bang that shook through the garage and house.

I skipped the prom.

In the passing blur of my senior year I looked up and found myself in a line of classmates, rehearsing for graduation in the severely narrowed funnel. I stepped aside, angering a teacher, who kicked me in the butt, and I got back in line.

That summer I was employed at an indoor ice rink where I took tickets, passed out skates, swept floors, painted locker rooms, sold pizza and hot dogs and pop and snowcones, hollered at misbehaving kids, ran errands, mowed grass. One of my jobs was to turn on the floodlights over the rink before the ice was resurfaced each morning. I swung open the door of the steel electrical box and pulled down a hefty gray switch, the ice sparkling in the blaze that surged from the power plant.

As I worked, I sometimes thought about the plant. I pictured the coal arriving by ship and train and truck, the black mountains beyond the towering belching smokestacks, the roaring dozers continually pushing the rolling heaps of coal toward the feeders of the Coal Building, and the coal pulverized and burned in the dim main plant where pressurized steam, heated to one thousand degrees Fahrenheit, turned the enormous whining turbines. I thought about my father reduced to small welding jobs at a table in the maintenance department, or, if he was in much pain that day, hidden by his kind foreman in a storeroom where the men in white shirts wouldn't notice that he was slumped in a metal chair, smoking cigarettes, popping yellow pills, moaning, doing no work, making no money for the power company, dying on company time while long dump trucks halted beneath the scrubbers of the smokestacks to load up with fly ash.

—————◆—————

Two weeks before my departure for college, my family squeezed into the Volkswagen and traveled to my going-away party at the Wagner farm. When we arrived, Grandmother was spreading a flowery plastic tablecloth on the long picnic table and Grandfather was preparing a charcoal fire in the red brick barbecue pit. April jumped out of the car and ran into the farmyard to join a cousin in chasing a hen out of the pig pen. Over the squawks and squeals and laughter, Grandmother screamed, "You stop that, you kids! You get on outta that pig shit right this second!"

Grandfather laughed. "The little buggers."

I couldn't wait to eat: grilled streak, roasted corn, potato salad, fresh tomatoes and scallions, fresh bread and homemade butter, warm apple pie heaped with vanilla ice cream. I snuck inside to raid the candy dish on the kitchen counter before announcing to the several adults sitting in lawn chairs that I was going fishing. Grandfather said, "You dasn't go far or you won't hear us when eats are ready. We'll have to give yours to the pigs."

"That's right," said Grandmother, glaring at him. "Wagner'll eat it himself." Then glaring at me, she said, "Don't fall in and drown. And if you do come back, don't track mud into my kitchen when you go sneaking more candy."

I sprayed on mosquito repellent and retrieved my fishing tackle and coffee can of worms from the car. Careful to avoid the tall nettle, I descended the steep muddy bank of Tonawanda Creek and sat down in the shade of a black willow. I cast the lead sinker and baited hook into the slowly swirling pool of a wide bend, and rested my rod on a forked stick pushed into the soft bank. I leaned back in the shade of the willow and watched the thin hanging leaves shimmer and shiver in the sunshine and breeze and was relieved to have escaped dutiful conversation with my elders.

In an hour I yanked merely one bullhead, flopping and gasping and bleeding, from its world. But then as I stood up to leave, the rod was jerked nearly double. I grabbed it just as it was about to streak into the creek and for a moment felt a great live weight at the end of the line, like that of the presumed sturgeon I once lost in the Niagara. This time it was likely that I had hooked a big carp. The line snapped. I threw down the pole and reflexively stepped forward after the escaped fish, nearly falling into the creek. Then I stood there at the edge of the water, and like the Chautauqua Lake fisherman who years earlier had lost the big musky, I screamed, "Fuck! Fuck! Fuck!"

Except for the soft sucking of the creek, there was silence. I stood still for a moment before collecting my gear. And as I climbed the steep slippery bank, I smelled the grilling meat and my stomach growled.

On the evening when I was beginning to pack for college, Dad called a family meeting. When we were all gathered around the kitchen table, he announced that Mom and he had been discussing what should become of the cabin after his death. She would need money, he explained, and the sale of the cabin would help. In our new home that fit me like an artificial limb, I had just learned that another leg of my past might be amputated. Immediately and vehemently, my sisters and I objected.

"Well," he said quickly, "I guess that about settles it—doesn't it, Eva?"

"I suppose."

During my last weekend before college, Dad finished work on the cabin. Earlier that summer he had finished laying stone up the front and sides of the fireplace, but had decided to face the backside with paneling instead of stone. The paneling would be the last building material we would carry into the cabin from the old pickup.

I helped him cut, lift into place, and nail down two sheets of the dark paneling, but he insisted on handling the third by himself. I stayed until he began to anger: "I told you I'll do it myself. Now go on. Go fishing or something. Go do something."

I asked him, "Why did you bring the pistol here?" He had brought the pistol with him and had set it, in its black holster, on the top shelf of the steel cupboard above the sink, and now his vehemence frightened me.

"The pistol? Oh—I just didn't want it in the house with April and her friends around. It's safer here."

"I'll stay and help you finish."

"Go on out."

"I'll just stay."

"Goddamnit. I told you to go outside."

I went out but could not make myself go far. When eventually I heard a sharp bang, a short squeaking cry escaped me, like the sound that a frightened frog makes as it leaps to water. I began to run back to the cabin before I realized that he was merely pounding in a nail. And suddenly my legs felt so weak that I had to sit down on the grass.

Freed of me, he had removed a small piece of charred hardwood from the fireplace and in carbon had written on the section of exposed fire brick:

This cabin
built by Jim Phillips in
the years of our
Lord 1966–1971

And with the remaining piece of paneling, he was covering up the inscription, sealing it with nails.

Because the pain was mounting in his back, I drove. Down the eight-hundred-foot gravel driveway and up the steep dusty road lined with Dad's weedy land on one side and a young conifer plantation on the opposite. Onto a narrow and bumpy and snaking macadam road and past two unbroken miles of hardwood forest on each side, rattling and bouncing down steep Yankee Hill as he groaned on the seat next to me. Onto School Street in little Ischua where there was no longer a school. Onto two-lane Route 16 north, the truck gaining speed beneath the drooping black power lines strung between the creosoted poles passing in a dark blur. Toward the power plant. Toward home.

Horace sits and listens. After the week of rain, the spring is surging as it did on his first night in the wilderness that is now a distant memory, a hazy dream. His visits to the spring are now rare. Someone has to take him there in the wagon and help him down and return to bring him back to the house. Sometimes he wanders off, and then they have to take time off from their work until he is found, lost in a field of tall corn or stranded in a steep ravine.

On the opposite hillside, his son William and a grandson and two great-grandsons sow oats. They and the soil and horses and wagon and sky are all swirling light and shadows and faint colors blurred by Horace's cataracts, dizzying him, and so he closes his eyes and listens. But his hearing is still good and he can hear the faint drifting voices of the boys on the hillside, and the sharp calling of the mating birds above him in the shade trees he transplanted five decades earlier, and the echoing of the shrieking train whistle off in Ischua Valley. And inches from his arthritic feet, the spring.

Are We Almost There Yet?

While the Volkswagen chugged in the middle of the narrow road in front of my dorm at Bloomsburg State College, I briefly embraced my parents.

"I love you," she said.

"You've made me proud, son," he said.

And I said, "See you later."

I hurried up to my stuffy room to watch my parents depart, but the Volkswagen was already out of sight when I reached the window out of breath. I saw car doors and trunks opening and closing and strangers lugging bulging suitcases. Beyond the clustered brick buildings and grassy slopes and small trees of the campus, the green hills were lusterless in the late August sun. I was ashamed of the way I had said good-bye. I made my bed and finished unpacking before again looking out the open window. Music spilled from the brick dormitories and rattled through the campus like dry leaves, and I wondered if I would ever see my father again.

Later that fall, Mom wrote to tell me that the cancer had resumed its spread. As I read her letter, I thought of the pistol, as if its solidity and heft made it a greater threat than the cancer that

219

appeared as a spilling shadow on X rays. And almost as soon as
I had put down the letter, I decided to move back home.

I wrote to the State University College at Buffalo, asking
how I might transfer.

The decorations were boxed and the brittle tree was dragged
into the field below the house, and Christmas was forgotten. In
the stiffening cold of January mornings my shuffling father
toted his lunch box to the icy car, my shivering bundled sisters
waited in the driveway for the school bus, and through a frosty
living room window I watched for my ride to college in Buffalo
as my mother in her heavy housecoat scrubbed the breakfast
dishes.

After taking notes on droning lectures that I'd paid for with
borrowed money, I rode home numbed. The route followed the
wide swift flow of the blue-and-white Niagara River. Then like
a reddish mountain, the brick walls of the power plant rose between the icy water and road, the thrusting stacks partially obscured in their own steamy oblong clouds, and the car was
veered onto an expressway that ran away from the plant and
river and toward Pendleton.

As the spring semester was ending, Dad informed me that the
power company would be hiring several college students for the
summer. They would work in the plant or with the traveling crews
who painted the high-voltage towers. The money would be better
than what I had earned at other summer jobs. Was I interested?

I didn't know much about painting towers, but I knew that
the plant was the dark hulking place that once sent my father

home so covered with coal dust that he was unrecognizable to me. It was the place that consumed so many of his evenings and weekends, leaving him exhausted and edgy, and I suspected that the plant had given him cancer. But my father and uncle and their father had gone to work there. Electricity was just in-efficient coal. Maybe it was my turn.

I needed the money.

I said yes.

I was assigned to the utility crew in the plant.

By July, my phlegm and snot were dark with fly ash and coal dust, my itching eyes constantly red, and often when I turned on a light at home I was reminded of my job and imagined I was still hearing the high whine of turbines or the rattle of coal falling through chutes. Yet whenever I swept one of the im-mense turbine rooms, I felt somewhat proud to know that all around me electricity was being generated for homes, factories, traffic signals, streetlights, hospitals. The sound of the turbines was intensely irritating, but I was soothed by recalling that my great uncles had helped build the original plant when Buffalo was still an important city, that my grandfather had helped ex-pand the plant before leaving ironwork to become a foreman there, and that my father at one time or another had helped re-pair each of the turbines that towered over my Sisyphean sweeping. Despite the nightmarish noise, filth, and heat, the plant could fill my head with a proud and foolish American dream. And although rumor had it that the company planned layoffs, I sometimes thought about applying for a permanent position.

Eventually I was transferred from the utility to the coal de-partment, where it became my responsibility to shovel up coal spills. The young grunts worked in utility and the lifers in maintenance, but the coal department possessed the walking wounded—and as often as not, the wounds were to the mind.

One of the workers was known as "Fuck It." Fuck It spent most of his time sitting on floors asleep, but every now and then he woke and glanced around, then flipped his wrist and said, "Fuck it." He had to watch where he sat though. Someone was taking great delight in dropping things on him from higher floors. At first it was water, but then it was lumps of coal, or nuts and bolts, which could be painful because Fuck It didn't wear his hard hat when he slept, sitting with his head drooped forward. He said the weight of the hard hat gave him a stiff neck. I didn't understand why he wasn't fired. Our foreman— who liked to read pornographic paperbacks in his office and frequently asked the men, "Hey, yuh got any dirty books for me?"—seemed to get a big kick out of waking Fuck It just to have him open his eyes in dazed surprise, smile, say "Fuck it" with his accompanying wrist gesture waving everything into oblivion, then go instantly back to sleep.

Another worker was known as "The Jerk": he was hyperactive but did no work. He spent most of his day walking about the plant complaining about the people and machines he passed. This usually started with a somewhat justified but vitriolic criticism that evolved into a stream of profanity lasting until another worker or machine caught his eye. When his complaining had exhausted him, he would break the lightbulbs in an obscure corner where he wanted to lie down. He took time not just to shatter the lights: he broke them off flush to the sockets. Perhaps the foreman got a kick out of him, too, because The Jerk was given the assignment of going to the cafeteria for lunch orders from our department. If someone ordered, say, a beef on weck, slice of apple pie, and black coffee, The Jerk would bring him back tomato juice, a pickle, and thirteen napkins.

Most of the other casualties in coal were hard workers—and one of them was known as "Mr. Work." Once during a rainstorm I looked out a grimy window and saw him shoveling around the coal feeders. He walked through puddles and was drenched. The stuff he was shoveling up was half coal, half water. And the water ran down Mr. Work's shovel handle into the sleeve of his one-piece work suit and exited from the bottom of his pants—black water.

The mountains were fiery when my father made his final visit to the cabin. I helped him out of the car. He shuffled to the building, gazing at the October foliage. I so needing to stretch my legs after the car ride that I forgot about the pistol and walked into the pines while Dad was alone in the cabin. I knelt and drank from the cold gliding spring. I hiked around the pond as rising trout left small ripples and bubbles where scores of flying ants struggled in the floating yellowish coating of pollen. With my arms raised above the goldenrod and ragweed, I started slowly down the overgrown dike toward the creek that swallowed the pond's overflow. But I turned back, itching and sneezing.

Then from the crest of the dike I was surprised to see thick smoke billowing from the chimney. Fearing that Dad had fallen asleep while smoking a cigarette, I ran sneezing the rest of the way around the pond and into the cabin.

On that warm afternoon my father had built a roaring crackling fire in the stone fireplace that had taken him five years to complete. He was sitting slouched on the couch, a lit cigarette in his shaky left hand, his forehead beaded with sweat. Without taking his eyes off the leaping flames, he said, "We'll wait until this burns down, then we'll start for home."

On the day that he retired from the power plant at age forty-five, Dad said, "I always hoped I'd live to grow old. Well, too bad. I have."

By January, the cancer was spreading like a subterranean coal fire. His moaning rose like smoke. I sometimes fled the sound by wandering my old neighborhood. Yet as I hiked Bear Ridge Road, I felt more misplaced than protected. Most of the boys I'd grown up with were away at college or laboring in southern factories, and some of our old play lots had been sold. The new owners were white-collar and planted thick hedgerows of spruce to shield the older and smaller homes from view.

The sparkling shallow snow squeaked beneath my insulated boots, and the frozen goldenrod crackled like fire, as if to mock my shivering. The wide drainage ditches were hard and windswept and the scattered trees occasionally boomed like an expanse of ice cracking in the Canadian gusts skating in off frozen Lake Erie. Yet regardless of how many miles I tried to travel into the past, I could neither escape nor forget the keening moaning of the present.

He waited in bed for his wife to deliver the meals and bedpans, his pained unused legs weakening until he could no longer walk. He waited for the growl of the yellow school bus that carried home a too-quick kiss from his younger daughter. For the canned guffawing of favorite television shows. For the gentle somewhat frightened hugs from his older kids. For the quiet visits from relatives and buddies who didn't know what to say. For his wife's hand soft on his forehead. In nearly unbearable pain he waited until they cut a nerve in his neck, paralyzing him from the waist down to kill the pain there. When he discovered that he hurt just as much in other places, that the pain in his legs had masked the other pain, his final decision was to take the morphine.

After that, the drug made all the decisions. Gradually he needed more and sooner morphine to satisfy a raving craving greater than the pain. His tired wife, who somehow was no longer his wife, injected into his withered ass and arms and legs his new fluid wife at whom he didn't need to shout.

He stopped eating.

One morning he hallucinated that an alligator was sunning itself atop the dresser. Then his old wife was at his bedside explaining that his catheter bag, whatever the fuck that might be, was filled with bloody urine. His son and a neighbor carried him out to the car. As the passenger door was opened, the neighbor said, "It's sure a cold day for spring."

Soon he found himself on a cart in a long bright hallway while people from his family—what were their names again?— talked to each other in worried tones. He shouted: he demanded his new wife.

Then he suddenly and shockingly needed something even more than his new wife. His eyes wide, he croaked, "I can't breathe."

He coughed up blood. His arms began waving around.

As his lungs filled with blood he felt in terror his life departing him while people in white were fast wheeling him into a room. Someone was trying to hold down his arms and the others were moving about uttering incomprehensible hurried words. Their whiteness melted and enveloped him and faded. A cold hard tube was shoved down his throat. He gagged. Everything was fading. Why had someone turned out the lights?

In complete darkness he heard a distant beating. Then that sound and all sound ceased. And the last thing he probably ever knew was that he was aloft in blackness and silence, his arms flapping with all the strength he had ever possessed.

Much of the route home from the hospital ran parallel to the river. I wondered, as my mother stared silently ahead in the passenger seat and as we passed the hulking power plant, why I wasn't feeling more grief. When had he died in us? Was it that day in the kitchen when he informed Kim and me that he had an incurable disease, that he wasn't immortal? When we watched the old family movies and he became violently sick on his final bottle of beer? When I embraced him so hard and long during our first time in Bloomsburg? When we last visited the cabin together? And for my mother was it the final time that they had sex? The first time that she injected him with morphine? I went on wondering until we were home.

We told Kim, who wept briefly and went into her bedroom. April wasn't awakened. Mom fell atop Dad's and her unmade bed, the door and curtains still open. Soon she was snoring. On the nightstand, a glass vial of morphine glinted in the moonlight.

The body was cremated. There was no funeral. We never picked up the ashes.

———⇒◆⇐———

After the man died who had kept the roof from leaking, I felt exposed. The rain seemed to pound harder and I studied the ceiling for leaks. At night my sheets felt moist, I shivered, pulled the blankets tighter.

For several weeks, I could fall asleep only by recalling the house we had lived in until I was sixteen. And even now I sometimes must resort to that old trick. In the reverie, I begin in the cellar. I run my fingers over the smoothly worn greasy wood of the workbench. Spin the fanged glinting blade of the table saw. Flail the dust from the punching bag. Switch off the lights and absorb the faint yellow escaping around the steel door of the oil furnace. Listen to water gushing from the drain spout and into the dark cistern. I feel my way up the narrow wooden stairs to the strip of white light under the door.

I stand for a minute in the hallway, my eyes adjusting to the full light pulsing from the plant where my father works. I listen to the high-pitched silliness of Saturday morning cartoons on the black-and-white television in the living room. To the clanging stirring of steaming tea by my nearly naked father who sits at the kitchen table and puffs a dangling cigarette. To the sudsy muffled rattling of my mother scrubbing yolk-smeared and greasy breakfast dishes in the white enameled sink. Heidi bounds clumsily up the hall, still a puppy with oversized feet. I glimpse my adult reflection in the wall mirror in the little bathroom across the hall. Suddenly I feel exhausted.

Wearing pajamas, I pad barefooted past my still-youthful parents who are beginning another day. No one speaks. I slowly climb the steep stairs to my bedroom, where cold rain pounds the roof and streaks down the rattling storm window. I slip beneath the clean sheet and thick quilt, and fall asleep. In a bed that is much softer and warmer than it ever was.

A year before he died, Dad and I began planting a thousand Scotch pine. But with barely a hundred seedlings set out in the abandoned pasture above the cabin, he stopped in pain and instructed me to plant the remainder in tangled clumps of fifty, the roots bare and damp, so that the trees might live until we could finish together on a weekend when he felt better. There would be no such weekend. And I would finish alone, a month after his death.

On the morning of the planting, I was glad to leave the cabin. Without my father's stories, the flames in the fireplace had seemed merely menacing. Without his struggling shuffles and winces and moans, the damp coolness of the concrete floor and block walls had made me feel, despite the fire, as if I were spending the night in a silent, dark, and waiting tomb. I gulped breakfast and was out into the cool early morning sunshine with my youth and planting spade. I was eager to recapture the feeling of immortality.

Almost all of the seedlings that Dad and I had planted individually were still alive. But of those planted in clumps of fifty, only two hundred or so seedlings had survived. I separated the roots of the living from the dead, then transferred the green seedlings into a bucket containing several inches of cold pond water.

I broke the frosty ground with the spade, inserted the first dripping seedling, stomped the dirt shut against the roots, and took two long strides before planting the next. The work and rising sun warmed me. I was sweaty and tired when I finished two hours later.

I stood and studied the corner of the field where I had just finished my father's work. Most of the seedlings were hidden from view by sprouting weeds, but here and there I could see the small and prickly head of an infant tree that Dad or I had planted. Because I didn't know that Scotch pine are relatively small and short-lived trees, I imagined them grown tall. And because I could still look into a mirror and detect no sign of aging, I imagined myself striding with taut skin and full dark hair into a towering forest that I had helped to plant.

I woke from a short nap wishing I had more seedlings to plant. After a cup of instant coffee, I strode to the pond with Dad's bamboo rod and fly box. The afternoon was sunny and breezy, laced with sharp birdsong, the pond sparkling and the creek loudly gushing. I caught two rainbows. I wished I had leeks to fry with the fish, and decided to gather some.

I located a leek patch in a maple woods near the cabin. I filled a bread bag with white acrid bulbs clumped with mud, then continued to hike through the woods. Thin snow lingered in the shade of hemlocks, slushy and dirty. But most of the forest was brighter, the hardwoods just beginning to leaf out, the snow gone.

Gnawing on the gaunt and muddy remains of a deer, an opossum glared and growled at me as I passed. The desperately hungry animal made me remember my father's hot stare and snarled words when he was overworked. And the power plant. And the cancer.

With sudden fright, I recalled the pistol. As if he could still kill himself. I started back to the cabin, using the shovel as a walking stick.

A little out of breath from my hurried return, I stood before the metal cupboard for several seconds. Then I opened the white painted door and saw, on the shelf where the pistol had been, a small jar of nuts and bolts, a scattering of dark mouse turds, and a coating of dust. I searched the rest of the cabin's single room, then the porch and attic, flinging things out of drawers and boxes as if looking for a lost and priceless heir-loom. But the pistol had been moved out of the cabin. And twenty-seven years would pass before I could discover where.

In the little cemetery atop Carpenter Hill, the lanky young preacher ad-
dresses the gathering, nasally and high-pitched: In the year of Our Lord
1825, Horace built a lean-to at a spring bubbling forth just as clean and
clear as Our Savior's love of the faithful. He spent that first lonely night in
black wilderness, far from his tender family, far from Christian civilization,
in a land then fit for but heathen savages. All night, the ravenous wolves
howled. Yet make no mistake—by day, Our Savior's sustenance bubbled
forth. The ravenous wolves were slain. Trees crashed down, and crops were
sown. Churches were raised. The faith and work of the noble pioneers bore
this fruit in the name of Our Lord.

His right arm extended dramatically, the preacher spins as he points at
fields and tame wood lots all around him. Dizzied, he almost falls into the
neat rectangular hole.

In the front row, Horace's son William covers his laughter with coughing. To take his mind off the preacher, he looks off into the distance at sheep
feeding on a steep hillside in tight clusters that look like patches of snow. He
notices a yellow crouching dog in the soggy pasture just beyond the cemetery. It creeps, stalking a woodchuck, then jumps up and charges as the
woodchuck lumbers to its burrow just in time. The rangy dog sticks its head
in the hole, digs with brief fury at the stony ground, then looks around and
trots off. Soon it disappears into the ravine of a stream that is running high
with last night's rain. William can hear the water.

The preacher begins to speak at length about Horace's character: he
was a devoted husband, a dear father, dotting grandfather and great-grandfather, a pillar of the church, a faithful servant of Our Savior. Then the
preacher pauses as he glances into the eyes of the mourners before him,

slowly shaking his head. With dripping paternal sadness, he adds, And unlike some of the professed Christians who stand here today on this hallowed ground, Horace Guild chewed not tobacco, gambled not with his earnings and children's bread, and drank not of poisonous spirits.

Several of the men in the crowd nervously clear their throats or cough and look down at their shifting feet while their wives nod vigorously. But for the second time that morning, William Guild smiles.

The shadow of a cloud drifts into the cemetery and women pull their shawls tighter and stoop to button their children's coats as the preacher talks about Judgment Day, heaven and hell, the eternal mercy and wrath of Our Savior. William shifts his weight from one foot to the other and wonders what became of the dog after it disappeared into the ravine. Maybe it caught something.

The preacher is becoming hoarse by the time he gets around to the subject of ashes and dust: And so we return the mortal body of our good Christian brother Horace Guild to this land that he and the other noble Christian pioneers made Christian for us all. His immortal soul is now in the hands of Christ. In the name of Our Savior. A-men.

⎯⎯⟩◦◦◦⟨⎯⎯

Later that afternoon, William Guild sits alone with his back against the ash that his father transplanted as a sapling. His father liked to say that the spring could speak, but William was never sure if Horace was being serious. For the first time since he was a boy, William leans back in the shade of the ash and closes his eyes and listens.

There Again

Two years after Dad's death, my mother married an apartment house landlord who had no interest in green hills or trout ponds. He wanted her to sell the cabin and land. She hoped I wouldn't mind. I did. So she deeded the property to me, glad, it seemed, to be done with that part of her life.

To feel worthy of my father's land, I continued to plant trees. Break the sod with a spade, insert the damp roots, stomp the hole shut, take three long strides, pry open the earth yet again: a thousand trees planted between sunrise and sunset. Pressing my muddy palms against my stiff lower back, I would pause in the spring dusk to survey my day's work and seasonal ritual and duty to the land I owned. The land that was taking ownership of me.

The woman I was dating offered to help me plant seedlings in the spring of 1976. We married in August. Margaret and I took unsatisfying jobs in Buffalo, where we rented a small hot apartment above a hair salon. We visited the cabin on every other weekend and during our vacations. Each spring we planted more trees.

During the summer of 1979, Margaret was offered a job teaching in an elementary school twenty miles north of the

233

cabin. We fell to packing. We stuffed clothing into grocery bags, dumped in clattering silverware, and dragged trashbags of superfluous documents and food and medicine out to the crumbling curb. We had neither a wrinkle nor gray hair between us, and were smitten with futurity, our lives opening before us like a route on a great unfolding map of forever.

I was going home to my father's cabin.

Even going home, people move forward. A hundred years ago, country women stitched pictograms on quilts to record marriages and births and deaths: a small white church, a blue infant, a black casket, as well as enigmatic symbols representing more personal events. But in the artificiality of my family photographs, everybody smiles like fools—even during the awful final weeks of Dad's life. Whenever I hunger for departed days, I find myself unsure where to hunt. What route follows time backward? I wish I had preserved the maps on which my father had traced routes from Pendleton to places where land was for sale: Great Valley, Short Tract, Knapp Creek, Cassaseraga, Kill Buck. The maps had become dirty and torn, and the route to Ischua was thick and ragged, as if he had retraced it each time he visited his cabin.

During the first weeks that Margaret and I lived at the cabin, our hearts were our only maps. In delight of the sun and moon, we sprung into the sparkling pond and up steep bright hills and under soft covers. At the start of our first full summer in the Alleghenies, I was in no hurry to find a job or even to prepare the cabin for winter.

On clear evenings we watched the sun settle behind the pasture on Seward Hill. After the birds roosted, we were amazed anew at the growing quiet and milky brightness far from city traffic and streetlights. But as gradually the starlight seemed to become too ancient in the deepening night, we apprehensively hurried inside to start a small fire.

We also loved those occasional evenings when lightning brightened the hanging knobby clouds. We remained out in the fast-darkening yard as thunder shook the thick air, but eventually a cool blast of wind smelling and tasting of rain would cause us to jump up from our lawn chairs. In bed I wrapped an arm around my young wife and nestled my face into her long thick hair. If we woke in grayness to a stormy morning, we might stay in bed for half the day, denned and content as water walked the roof.

Then one morning I woke to Margaret getting ready for her first day of work. And a few dawns later, when I went outside to pee, the grass crunched coarse and silvery beneath my bare feet, which burned as I went back inside. That night I dreamt that an ice storm had caused damage I was too infirm to repair: gutters down and tree limbs through the cabin roof. The dream triggered a flurry of home improvement. I had good reason to hurry: far from the road, in hills where winter was severe, we had moved into a one-room cabin without electricity or running water. I had spent the summer lulled by the singing of birds that were now flying south.

First I insulated the ceiling. Next I piped springwater into a twenty-gallon plastic garbage can set into the ground between the cabin and pond; then from the can I ran a pipeline to a pitcher pump bolted to a low shelf in the cabin. I converted a small closet into a shower by mounting a large sink on concrete blocks and by bolting a second pitcher pump to a wooden shelf about five feet above the sink. We stood in the sink and showered by pumping warmed water up from a five-gallon pail set beneath the elevated sink; the waste water drained into a different pail. The cabin already had a propane stove and lights, and I added a propane refrigerator. Finally, my uncles Al and Fred and I installed a wood stove that would produce more warmth than the fireplace, while burning much less wood. After firing up the stove for the first time, I passed out beer and said to my father's brothers, "Well, now I'm ready for winter."

"So you're really going through with this?"

"My grandmother says we'll only do this one winter."

"She thinks you'll last a whole winter?"

I was consumed by a sort of blood-and-fruit lust for living off the land. Totting burlap sacks over the hills, I gathered bushels of wild apples and berries. I canned juice and jelly and I baked pies. Cider fermented in an oak whiskey barrel out in the yard. By then I owned a hunting dog, a Labrador retriever that flushed birds and rabbits before my gun. I canned the meat for winter meals.

The best hunting places were near the small drywall foundations of abandoned houses, where game fed on the elderberries and apples and shriveled grapes still clinging to the crumbling domesticated past. Grouse whirred quick like noisy blurry ghosts from overgrown vineyards. Rabbits zigzagged fast to burrows dug near drywall foundations. From the sogginess of old drainage ditches, lance-beaked woodcocks flew straight up before fatally pausing in the blue light of a frosty morning to choose a direction of escape. One morning I was so surprised by a flock of turkeys that I missed the first to flush from an abandoned apple orchard. I killed the second. With her tail blurred in ecstasy, the dog fetched the ten-pound hen, dragging it by the neck through a clawing patch of briars.

On the opening day of deer season, I ate sausage and eggs for breakfast, an opening-morning ritual of my father's. I was in the woods well before daylight. The buck I killed that day was the biggest I'd ever seen. Margaret and I stayed up all night cutting the meat into stew-sized chunks for canning. I fried venison for my breakfast as soon as we finished the butchering, but Margaret had become sickened by the hours of sharp knives and sticky blood and wouldn't eat meat for two weeks.

I was so glad to have shot such a large buck that I had forgotten to perform over the slain deer the primitive ritual of asking the spirit of the animal for forgiveness. Weeks later, when I told this to a Native American I knew, he asked, "Do you have rheumatism?"

"In each of my big toes."

"Now you know why."

I couldn't tell if he was making fun of me. But I did know that Margaret thought it foolish to ask a dead deer for forgiveness. "If you feel you need forgiveness," she asked, "why do you hunt to begin with?"

My days depart. And I hunt in delight of the sun and moon: in delight of fruit and blood.

A hundred feet below the steep place on the hillside where the spring slipped from beneath the hollow white ash, the land became briefly level. On the level place was a mossy slightly sunken rectangle that looked like the old site of a small building. I asked the town historian if it was the site of a log cabin. She wasn't sure. She told me that the first settler on my land was Horace Guild, who had made his journey into the wilderness with his friend David Hibner. Guild built a temporary cabin somewhere in the forest and began clearing land for farming. He eventually moved into a frame house along a trail that would become a county road. Two of his sons died in the Civil War, but he himself lived a long life. He was buried in tiny Carpenter Hill Cemetery, where the living have a lovely view of the surrounding fields and forested hills. The rest of his story I imagined as I sat in the shade of the hollow ash and sipped hard cider. Or heard it from the murmuring spring that chilled the jars of cider.

Throughout Margaret's and my first winter at the cabin, I read about the Allegheny pioneers. They had built small log cabins with floors of split basswood, open-hearth fireplaces of stone gathered from creek bottoms, and chimneys of sticks and mud. Large families lived in those dim smoky drafty cramped dwellings until they could afford to build a frame house. Or until they gave up, cast out by the promised land to return emaciated to civilization. During the warm months, the crops frequently failed or were consumed by insects, blight, and wildlife. Large predators stalked the free-foraging livestock. Then from November to April it snowed, food became scarce, and people fell ill. The older cemeteries in Ischua are full of the decayed victims of ague, yellow fever, smallpox, and dysentery, and mothers who died during childbirth and babies who were still-born. With the ghostly wolf at the door, it's small wonder that the men hunted down the corporal wolf with such fury. In his old age, surely pioneer Guild sat at the spring and listened and remembered. Surely he drank to survival.

Such historical accounts made the worries and warnings of my relatives seem foolish. Margaret and I would not be threatened by starvation, smallpox, or cougars. When pressed, my relatives couldn't identify a specific hazard of my becoming "a hillbilly hermit," as my grandmother had put it. But they were certain that no good could come of living without a telephone and electric blanket and pop-up toaster. "Anyhow," my mother insisted, "won't you be bored without a TV?"

She was onto something there. Although in modern accounts of going Thoreau, some of the authors describe winter depressions and rage brought on by long snowy confinements, the male pioneers of the Alleghenies, and many of the women, too, spent their days outside regardless of the season. During winter, if they weren't hunting game, they were clearing land for spring planting. The felled hemlock were stripped of the tannin-rich bark, the hardwoods were burned for potash, and the white pine were sledded to large streams so that the logs could be floated to mills. To the pioneers, cabin fever would have been a luxury. But it was a luxury that Margaret and I could afford.

By then I was employed at a rural home for delinquent boys. But except when my wife and I were away earning paychecks, we were confined to the twenty-by-twenty-five-foot cabin. Cabin fever drifted in under the door like the plague.

As the snow deepened outside the cabin one night, Margaret asked me how I could stand to keep reading about the pioneers, or as she put it, "so much on one subject." Her gum crackled. I didn't answer her question, and she asked why we didn't talk anymore. I shrugged. The irritating crackling was becoming louder. I suspected that she was making the noise on purpose because she was jealous of my being outside clearing land and hunting with the pioneers while she was stuck inside. She was probably happy when a page ripped as I turned it. Out in the darkness, the snow fell and swirled. A growing drift pressed against the picture window.

After the storm, we had to leave Margaret's car and my Jeep at the end of our eight-hundred-foot driveway and carry our groceries and laundry through the deep snow. Friends and neighbors no longer visited. In the mornings, we usually needed to shovel our vehicles out of deep lumpy snow that had been hurled by the night plows. Often one or both of the engines wouldn't start. Each of us stayed later and later at work. In the cabin we spoke little but eyed each other with furtive hope, as if embarrassed to be searching for signs of spring in January.

On a sunny morning in late February, the snow began to melt around the black piles of deer dung and the dark rough bases of cherry and maple trees. I strapped on snowshoes, and set off through the blinding hills. I pulled myself up the steeper slopes by gripping saplings, then half snowshoed and half slid down the opposite slopes. In the narrow ravines I carefully crossed the frozen streams where the tracks of hunting mink suddenly appeared or disappeared at breaks in the windswept ice. I squinted, and felt my face tanning.

I began to track a fox. Each fur-blurred footprint was in line with the previous where the fox had traveled straight from vole

colony to vole colony. But it had twice circled a hidden bait and
trap. I knew the trap was there because earlier that winter, when
the snow was still shallow enough for her to plunge ahead without becoming exhausted, my dog was caught in it while we
hunted grouse. Although she was uninjured, my first impulse
after freeing her was to destroy the trap. But I didn't. I preferred
the forest the way it was: doom and hope covered by the same
snow.

When my thighs began to ache from the high swinging gait
of snowshoeing, I started to loop home. Eventually I came upon
my own tracks filling with snow fleas milling and hopping in
the sunshine, and nearing the cabin I saw sap bleeding from ice-
damaged maples. I pictured the busy Allegheny sugar bushes
where tin buckets were drumming with fast-dripping sap as
farmers hurried to finish the drilling and tapping.

Back on the yard of the cabin, I built a snow wife. I made a
foray into the house, then strapped a bra over the sculpted
breasts. And when a snowball splattered against the back of my
head, I knew that Margaret, the warming one, had joined me
outside for a day of promise.

When true spring arrived in April, Margaret and I were
wakened early each morning by geese landing on the pond with
a great honking and splashing. They kept up the welcome
racket all morning, the trumpeting and hissing males challeng-
ing each other with snaky necks stretched low over the cold
water. When we arrived home from our jobs on calm and sunny
afternoons, we could hear the purring of bees at the blooming
pussy willows that fringed the pond like sweet tassels.

Later that spring, my mother spent a night at the cabin to help Margaret and me plant conifer seedlings early the next morning. Instead of using the wood stove that night, I built a fire in the fireplace. While we watched the flames, Mom asked if I'd ever found Dad's pistol.

I had trouble falling asleep that night, wondering again what had become of the pistol after Dad had moved it from his bedstand to the cabin. Then around midnight I woke to drawers and cupboards quietly opening and closing. For a moment I thought I was back in Pendleton: Dad yanking open the bedstand drawer, fingering the weapon in the darkness, pushing the drawer shut, opening it again a few minutes later. In the morning, Mom said that she had been unable to sleep and had been looking for something to read. But I knew that she had been searching for something else, had needed to know what had become of the weapon.

By nightfall, my wife and mother and I had planted two thousand trees.

I took a teaching job. From July to September, Margaret and I sunned and daydreamed and read on blankets out on the lawn, swam in the pond, napped whenever we felt like it. On sultry afternoons, I sought relief in the shady pocket of cool air near the spring. Sitting on the arching root of the hollow ash, I sipped hard cider and recalled Dad running his cool, dripping hand over my brushcut: "Yep, Mark, we're gonna have lots of good times here." It had been his idea that I become a teacher, and there I was at the cabin, a teacher married to a teacher, my summers off, having an easy good time. If he had lived, he still would have been welding in the power plant.

On cooler mornings, I took long hikes. When I returned to the cabin, I felt like I'd time traveled, and not just because my arthritic big toes made me feel like an old man. In the Alleghenies, the past and present and future drifted about with the ease of cloud shadows. On the land once farmed by Horace Guild and his family, on hillsides throughout the Alleghenies, and even on the fertile farmland in the valleys, the ancient forest was returning of its own will. The centuries insisted on mingling.

Humans flattered themselves with the fairy tale that they had permitted the reforesting of nearly twenty million acres of the Northeast. But trailing leafy mud and black smoke over the steep back roads, the logging trucks still rumbled and growled to and fro like so many Beelzebubs. Meanwhile, the forest continued to spread of its own firm and dreamy will. And I saw that even if the loggers, developers, farmers, and air polluters destroyed the trees until they could no longer grow back, some other invisibly driven wildness would take the place of the forest. A glacier or desert or radioactive mold dreamed by the land, watered by time.

A hike of any distance took me past mossy piles of stones gathered a century earlier from farmed land that was now forested, and past overgrown foundations where every scrap of lumber had rotted away. On wooded land that had once been farmed, I imagined a sweaty draft horse leaning into the leather plow harness, a field of winter wheat rippling in the wind, a house and barn surrounded by stumps. Crossing recently abandoned pasture, I imagined the thick mossy boles of the virgin forest that had once grown there, or how the land would look when overtaken by second-growth forest.

Abandoned roads were sometimes my trails. A short distance from the cabin, Whiterite Road had become a muddy farm lane intersected by Taylor Road, which was grown up with forest. The former residents of the Whiterite and Taylor roads had long ago moved into the little cemeteries atop Yankee and Carpenter hills, their gravestones worn blank by a century of wind and rain. Some of the buried had helped cut the virgin forest, dooming most of the wildlife that had not been shot or trapped. But bears were once again roaming the reforested Alleghenies. A new canine, a wolf-coyote hybrid known as the eastern coyote, was filling the niche of the exterminated timber wolf. Two of my neighbors claimed to have seen cougars. I was glad about the spread of the coyotes and hoped that cougars were indeed returning to the Alleghenies: deer were so populous that they were stripping the second-growth forest of all ground vegetation except the unpalatable ferns.

Although I was happy about the return of the wild, I felt bad for an ex-farmer I knew. He spoke of his land with the hurt of abandonment. "See that hillside up there? You can't see much of the ground anymore, but kinda steep. Maybe you been up hunting. A little steep and stony, but good corn land anyhow. Made a lot of silage. And now look at her: almost a woods already. Now it's the deer and coyotes do the harvesting."

One family in Ischua still owned the compass that had pointed their pioneer ancestors through the wilderness. On another family's barn wall, some ancestor had hung the yoke of the oxen that had pulled the plow that had first broken the soil of a farm now haunted anew by wild canines. From old porches,

retired farmers looked out over a land of echoes, as if the heir-
loom compass had led the generations in a big circle.

Whenever I returned sore-footed and sweaty from long
hikes, I got down on my hands and knees and drank like a deer
from the spring. Slurped until the cold stabbed my head. My
father used to brag to the guys at the plant that his spring ran 43
degrees for most of the year, and even in summer warmed to
only 46 degrees. They kept telling him that he needed to buy a
new thermometer, so he did, but the new one also showed that
the water was 46 degrees in the middle of July. I once contacted
a government geologist to ask why the spring stayed so cold
while two nearby springs became warmer during the summer.
The scientist speculated that the water might flow up from an
ice cave.

Leave your hand too long in that water, and you lose it.

During the first several years that Margaret and I lived at the
cabin, our families contracted and expanded like a pair of lungs.
Grandfather Wagner died from a stroke. Margaret's mother and
my mother's second husband died from cancer. Three of Margaret's grandparents died from one cause or another. My sister
Kim suffered renal failure, and she died from a hospital infec-
tion after I gave her one of my kidneys. But Margaret's four sisters had several babies between them.

I saw a hawk rip a squirrel from a spruce in our yard. A doe
suckled a fawn on the steep pasture opposite the cabin. Wild de-
ciduous saplings came up fast between the rows of conifers I
had planted with my father and mother and wife. My hair
began graying and falling out. I sometimes wondered if my
father would still recognize his land, or me. Margaret and I

woke late at night to the loony yipping and eerie howling of eastern coyotes. We talked about having children.

My map kept unfolding into the Alleghenies.

When a carpenter removed the warped paneling from the back wall of the fireplace, he uncovered the inscription that my father had made as he had finished work on the cabin. When I saw it, I reached out to touch the black words: "This cabin built by Jim Phillips." My fingers felt only the cool coarse firebrick, but the rest of me felt as if I had been visited by Dad's ghost. I pictured him stooping in pain to write on the brick with a piece of charred wood, and I wondered why he had covered up the inscription. Perhaps he had believed that I would one day uncover it, a posthumous gift. I asked the carpenter to leave it exposed.

When the builders finished work, only the fireplace was recognizable as part of my father's cabin. The original building had become a small living room and small bedroom joined to an addition consisting of a kitchen, bathroom, and second bedroom. And the house had electricity and running water. I was delighted to read in brightness instead of by grainy propane light, to take a shower without working a pitcher pump, and to sit on a flush toilet instead of over the fetid pit of a chilly outhouse. Yet I felt guilty. My father's inscription on the back of the fireplace caused me to recall his emphatic pronouncement as he had described the cabin he was planning to build: "And absolutely no goddamn power company electric!"

I had held out until my pregnant wife had said, "Fine. We don't need electricity or running water. But you'll be in full charge of diapers." So I had given in, telling myself that it would be neglectful to raise children without modern conveniences. It was absurd to feel guilty about using electricity, but I still thought of my cabin as my father's cabin.

As I used the new lights and appliances, I sometimes pictured the black branching power lines strung from pole to pole between the plant and my two childhood homes. Dad was at the source of the power. Trapped in darkness, he screamed unheard while a man wearing a white shirt, up in the bright and air-conditioned control room, prepared to fire up the imprisoning boiler. I remembered the fly ash and coal dust and welding fumes laced with poisons, the castration, the searing pain stronger than morphine, and my father's arms waving as he gasped for air that wouldn't come. And occasionally, when the clean suave newsman on television reported that the Dow Jones Industrial Average was up or down, I would say, "You sonofabitch."

Margaret would say, "I don't think he can hear you."

Nor had he heard my father.

I thought a lot about Dad while Margaret was pregnant, a father-to-be contemplating the father-who-was. As I traced routes from the past, I believed that I understood some of the coal-black and electric-bright American dream in which my father had labored, why his job had scorched his moods, and how the plant might have generated his death. I also believed that I understood the trapped sense of duty that had led him to work overtime and to say yes to castration.

Other men in my family had been possessed by the same duty. They came home exhausted from their jobs, and some came home in pain, or in pine boxes. Two of my great-uncles fell to their deaths on the job. Two of Grandpa Phillips's ribs were broken, and one of Grandfather Wagner's ankles. Welders have a higher rate of prostate cancer than do other men. Yet though their jobs were threatening and sometimes humiliating, these men were Sisyphean proud: they provided their children with sustenance, comfort, and a future. Sometimes a fatherless future.

I had forgiven my father for his searing glares and even for his stinging belt. And for the silent treatment that had now lasted for over a decade.

But there was one thing I still didn't understand about him. Near the end, when duty had been met and the pain of his illness had become nearly unbearable, what had kept him from using the pistol? In the safety of my good health, I wondered if he didn't have enough bravery. Or had too much. I felt that I couldn't know without first locating the pistol, as if it could tell a story or would at least offer a clue. But Mom had searched our old home in Pendleton, and both of us had searched the cabin. And although the builders had uncovered my father's sooty proclamation on the back of the fireplace, they had not uncovered a hidden gun or secret map.

I got it in my head that the gun had been overlooked. "Maybe it's down inside the couch somewhere. The couch has been here since he was alive."

"You looked there," said Margaret, in a tightly stretched maternity dress. "You told me you looked there."

"Maybe not carefully enough."

"It's gone."

"What if the baby finds it someday? What if it's loaded?" I tossed aside the cushions, slipped my hands into the dirty crevices below the armrests, flipped the couch upside down, shined a flashlight over the rusty springs and frame. My search became progressively irrational. I examined the ceiling and fireplace for signs that a stone or piece of plaster had been removed and sealed back into place. I examined the outside walls of what had been the cabin, searching for a hidden cavity large enough for a pistol. I hurried to the spring and peered up into the hollow ash.

After I could think of nowhere else to search, I made my way to the end of the rotting dock. Beyond the dike, the land dipped into a wooded ravine cut by a stony stream, then rose into a stubbly hayfield. A woodchuck plodded to its hole as a hawk kited in the blue. Barreling parallel to the crest of the field, a milk truck threw up a plume of dust where the gravel road hugged a forested hillside. I looked out over the water and land and into the sky, the green fading into the pause of September, the blue brightening in the chill. And I stopped fretting about Dad and about Margaret's bursting womb and the kind of father I might be. A few feet from the dock, a trout leapt for a glittery blue damselfly: a silvery twisting instant smacking into shards of water and dreamy light.

My Father's Cabin

The pistol is tucked in the stiff black leather holster hanging from his belt as he steps to the end of the short dock. He looks beyond the pond and the weedy earthen dike. He spies a woodchuck on the mowed land rising from the brushy ravine below the pond, fattening on the grasses and clover near its hole. He sees it rise onto its hind legs, searching the land for foxes and the sky for hawks, but on this cool still morning moment, the hayfield is empty of predators and the sky, after two drizzly foggy days, is empty of everything except the rising sun.

The woodchuck drops back to all fours. The man's eyes follow the lifting slope of the land as the pasture meets the muddy road and then keeps rising, forested and steep. He sees that the high fringes of the maples are beginning to turn color. Surrounded by the lusterless green of the beeches and birches, the bright splashes of red remind him of the embers when he rose from bed and knelt before the fireplace, leaned forward, and revived them with his breath. He sees the mist rise from the pond and feels it creeping up his loose pant legs. He feels the rising sun warm his face. He feels the weight of the bolstered pistol solid at his side.

Then he leaves the dock, a loose board springing beneath his steps. He begins to circle the water. Two Canada geese stretch their long necks, lifting and turning their heads, but stay where they are in the middle of the pond. They make no sound as he follows the shoreline, limping slightly and stop-

251

ping every so often to rest and to study the water and pines and sky. He sees trout swimming almost to the surface to take emerging mayflies, the water swirling and rippling. A long rainbow rises so close to him that he is startled by the sucking of the water as the fish swings downward with its prey in an orange and silvery flash. He sees newts floating just beneath the surface, and wonders why the trout do not take them also.

Where the spring slips into the pond, he stoops and puts his right hand in the icy water for a moment. Although on this morning his pain is faint, he straightens with a habitual moan and grimace. A plump green frog splashes into the pond and darts along the bottom, trailing a thin cloud of mud. When the man has circled back to the springy dock, he again steps out to the end.

He stands for a while without moving, on the weather-beaten boards. Then he looks down toward his faintly aching right hip and with his right hand slowly lifts the pistol from the stiff black holster. He holds the gun before him and studies it for a moment before slowly swinging back the hand gripping the butt, until behind his back his arm is stretched out parallel to the dock. Then he quickly swings the arm and hand forward, and releases. For an instant the pistol neither rises nor falls, spinning at its apex beneath the blue sky before it arches down and splashes into the water and disappears from view and comes to rest where it will stay until the pond is drained for cleaning three decades later. The geese honk and beat their wings on the water as they rise, necks outstretched, the racket growing frantic.

For over a minute he keeps his right arm and hand where they were when the pistol was released. Then the arm begins to shake and he lowers the hand to his side. He concentrates on exactly which muscles are tired and trembling. He listens to his breathing. And there near the cabin he built, standing on the narrow springy dock, shifting his weight from one foot to the other, he watches the water calm.

My father thinks, I wouldn't have seen this.